THIS BOOK IS FOR YOU IF...

- You are going through a marital crisis
- Your life has lost meaning
- You want to feel happy again
- If you have lost everything financially
- If you are a woman with more responsibilities than you should have
- If you want to get in touch with your greatness and find your purpose
- If you have lost a child
- If you are an entrepreneur

WHAT PEOPLE ARE SAYING

My mother raised three children on her own, so I'm a little partial to superhero moms like her and Paula Morelos Zaragoza. (Paula is also rising three children on her own: one of them with special needs). Her new book will inspire anyone who faces adversity and needs to be reminded of the power they possess.

Randy Gage, New York Times bestselling author and international speaker.

They say everything in life is a choice. What if they never told you that and when you learned it you had no choice but to choose what life just put in front of you? Then life itself becomes a door of discovery, growth and wisdom. That is what makes "Bulletproof Woman" a fascinating journey. Paula is a woman whose story may have much in common with yours, but when she tells it, you not only feel it and live it, you understand that, to bring to life the most important part of your essence, the BEING that lives in you, you need to face the darkest, the most fearful, but what eventually sets you free. This book is a testament that Paula, and every woman, possesses the qualities to bring out that warrior, that Valkyrie, that lives in them, to leave a mark on this world.
Inspirational, touching and very practical pages that can be turned into tools for your life. Thank you for giving us this gift.

Jorge Meléndez, coach and author of the book "Not Know: the path to unlearn".

The first time I heard Paula's story I thought two things: "It is incredible that this woman has come out ahead with everything that happened to her" and "all women in the world should know her story". I am glad that finally the book where she tells it has seen the light Every woman who wants to move forward with her life and doesn't know where to start should read it.

Jaime Lokier, author of the bestsellers Leadership Networks and Leaders Die (Movements Don't).

A book that reflects the essence of Paula: loving, intelligent, direct and courageous. A story full of revelations so honest that they immediately connect with our soul and recommendations so valuable that we want to take notes from the first page. Thank you, Paula, for inspiring us to believe, to discover and create that extraordinary being, that "Bulletproof" man or woman that already lives inside each one of us.

José López, coach and entrepreneur.

If you like the idea of exploring life and becoming aware of how the stories, we tell ourselves can limit or define us, this is the book for you. Paula inspires us to tap into our hearts and access our personal power with her authentic, energetic and resilient storytelling in the face of challenges.

I resonated and connected with her invitation: to live boldly and committedly by discovering that all that we want to be is already in me and in you, from this recognition we can hold each other with respect, love and trust... we become unstoppable.

Brenda Quintana, Author of the book "Sana Suelta Sigue", Women Empowerment Coach and creator of the Women in the Spotlight Program.

About the Author

Paula Morelos Zaragoza Wiechers. She has a degree in Journalism. Communication Intelligence Specialist. Lecturer. Radio broadcaster. Writer.

Author of **BULLET PROOF WOMAN, Live your truth and return to your being and Women empowered from their being, a New Feminism Manifesto.**

Creator of the Podcast **Bullet Proof Woman**, dedicated to the accompaniment and empowerment of women.
She was born in Mexico City in the early seventies and went through a challenging childhood living in a monoparental family with no economic resources.

he has an exciting history involved with mental illness, the loss of a child, bankruptcy, raising three kids by herself, and dealing with her youngest daughter's Down Syndrome.

She is a born communicator and passionate about the female gender to whom she has dedicated most of her professional work, helping women to discover that we are all called to greatness and to rediscover the colors of life.

Dedication

To Nicole, María and Lucía, source and reason for all my inspiration and desire to be a better woman.

Acknowledgements

I am deeply grateful to every teacher and guide I have had throughout my life.

To Alicia, my mother, who since I was a child planted in me the seed of curiosity for knowledge and to form my own criteria.

To my sister Iona, for whom I have always wanted to be better and who has shared with me this path towards finding our essence and the way back to our Self.

To my daughters Nicole, María and Lucía, who despite all our struggles always give me a big smile and all the support I need.

To Mercedes Martínez, Jaime Lokier, Jorge Meléndez (what a team!), mentors who have inspired and guided me, step by step, since I began to see the light.

To my friends and fellow entrepreneurs with whom, shoulder to shoulder, we have overcome every difficulty to make our way in the pursuit of our dream.

Each one of you is part of the Bulletproof Woman I am today.

Index

Acknowledgments	8
Introduction	11
Chapter 1 | Apocalypse	16
Chapter 2 | Bulletproof Woman	27
Chapter 3 | Your Limit	33
Chapter 4 | Hands on	42
Chapter 5 | Responsibility	57
Chapter 6 | Purpose	66
Chapter 7 | Serving	74
Chapter 8 | Balance	82
Chapter 9 | Decision	93
Chapter 10 | Perseverance	101
Chapter 11 | Commitment	109
Chapter 12 | The Birth of a Valkyrie	115
Chapter 13 | Your Life Happens Today	120
Epilogue	128
From my library to you	130
About the Author	131
Concluding Remarks	132
Additional Resources	134
The Dragonfly	136
The Valkyrie Code	137

Pubished by
Filament Publishing Ltd
14, Croydon Road, Beddingtom
Croydon, Surrey CR0 4PA   UK
+44 (0)208 688 2698
www.filamentpublishing.com

©2022 Paula Morelos Zaragoza Wiechers
ISBN 978-1-915465-10-8

All rights Reserved
No portion of this work may be published without
the advanced written permission of the author

The right of Paula Morelos Zaragoza Wiechers to be
identified as the author of this work has been asserted
by her in accordance with the Designs and Copyrights Act
1988 Section 77.

Introduction

This story begins at the base of a mountain, imposing and mystical. One that, when I was young, I did not like as a companion and certainly did not understand all that it meant. A place where I did not choose to live, where I was taken against my will. My immature will and full of young and wrong ideas. It was at the base of that mountain that I picked up a book for the first time. I read because there was nothing else to do. There was no internet, no cell phones. We didn't have a phone line or an open TV antenna at home. There were only books. Some with topics that caught my attention, others not so much, but, in this situation, I read everything there was available, so I won´t go crazy.

Life went by very slowly in that Magic Town. A town full of stories and strange people, out of the ordinary. Undoubtedly a unique and enigmatic place.

As the months and years went by, I managed to get in tune with all its mysticism and stories.
It was in this context that I got my hands on the fabulous story of The Hobbit by JRR Tolkien, followed by The Lord of the Rings trilogy. I spent many weeks glued to those books. I read day and night. There were days when I did nothing else. I would turn the pages until I fell asleep, longing for the next day to continue.

I remember so many moments under my window and outside, the dark night. I lived every story detail as if it was really happening. I don't think I have experienced another time in my life when my imagination was on 24 hours a day. I dreamed the story, ate the story, laughed and cried the story. I felt part of that world.

And I began to become passionate about all kinds of fantastic subjects and develop a passion for reading. I dreamed of one day writing my own fantasy story. I felt a genuine passion for letters, I filled notebooks with different short stories and thoughts that filled my head. Writing them down gave me peace.

It seems to me that many of the events recounted in those books reminded me of the anxieties, overwhelming and challenging moments of my childhood. Of course, there I could attribute them to people and then they didn't hurt. I could see them from the outside, as a spectator. It was much easier to understand all of it.

It was then that I knew I wanted to be a writer. A storyteller. Writing would be my form of expression and my catharsis, when I needed to process things, experiences, memories.

Each of the stages described throughout this saga clearly describe the "Hero's Journey" described by Joseph Campbell. It is only at this moment I have really become aware I have lived this journey step by step throughout my life.

At that age, at seventeen, the yearning to write a book was born in my heart. A book that would tell my own stories. And the overwhelming truth is that today, exactly thirty years later, all the puzzle pieces have come together, and I finally feel free to write without having to think too much about what I am sharing. Each stage of my life with its very good and very bad experiences has given me the self-credibility I needed to put together this writing for you.

I have had this book brewing in my head for too long. The funny thing is today when I sit down to write, the stories are completely different. None of the ones I had originally captured. And the fact is that all those initial stories have been healing one by one over the years and are part of who I am.

Writing, expressing ourselves, telling our truth, is a catharsis that many of us need to feel free.
I am really happy to realize that our story is organic, it changes constantly, just as the reality in which we saw it does. The only thing that is constant is change. Everything we experience every day, the little or much we learn from our experiences and the small and large modifications we are able to make, make us evolve.

This book is my proposal, my collaboration to give you some elements to help you realize things, to open your eyes, to begin to change and grow. To grow in wisdom and knowledge.

May you change so much that the friends you have stopped hanging out with feel they have to know you again.

The intricate adventure of telling my story, or at least some of its scenes, has connected me with my deepest essence and for that I am deeply grateful to the heroine in me. For finally daring to fight all her demons without stopping. For assuming herself as what she is, as what I am: A Valkyrie warrior who through these letters will show you the most honest part of her being.

I will describe the Valkyrie as a symbol and why it is an important part of my identity.

In history, these Nordic maidens of Viking origin were represented as young and beautiful, with glowing white arms and flowing golden hair.

These brave women had the role of rescuing wounded soldiers and were in charge of caring for them and nurturing them until they were able to get back on their feet and take their place on the battlefield.

Besides the fact that in my dreams I like to visualize myself as this young and beautiful maiden, the element that hooked me on these symbolic women was that they were not engaged in frontal fighting but were all the other warrior's support. Brave enough to go into the middle of the fight to rescue the wounded and bring them to safety.

I feel that way today. I visualize myself like this. Strong, brave, full of life and connected to the most powerful source of energy, that of the earth. An energy capable of renewing everything. To give life again after floods, fires, earthquakes and cataclysms. The earth always renews itself; it has that capacity. And you, me and every person who inhabits it have this capacity too.

I will share with you how this process of awareness, awakening, rebirth and evolution has changed me. I will tell you how I became a Bulletproof Woman.

Chapter 1 | Apocalypse

Five o'clock in the morning. I opened my eyes to another day. Like every day for the past two months, I had to run to the bathroom to throw up. Bitter bile. It was just bile. Lately it was the only thing my body was producing, triggered by an anguish that was already beyond my capacity. I couldn't stop thinking about the million things that tormented me and took away my peace.

Peace... It had been a long time since I had experienced it, in fact, it had become my greatest yearning. To be able to live in peace, to be able to live a day without starts, without surprises, without overwhelming events.

The phone started ringing early in the morning. Calls from banks and creditors, demanding payment. One after another. Threats of repossession. Not subtle reminders that I was in the middle of a chaos of epic proportions.

I felt the weight of the world on my shoulders, and it hurt physically. My face and my body rictus reflected a woman with many more years than I had. How to hide the wear and tear and emotional exhaustion? The body does not lie and always shows how we are inside. At this point I felt I had lived ten lives in one. And to top it off, I was experiencing a mid-life crisis.

I kept thinking that I needed to make a radical decision. I was slowly losing my mind. My understanding was completely clouded. But how could he go through this, if he was not well? I had not one, but three young daughters. If I didn't have a penny to make my way. If everything scared me to death.

If I was so tired, strengthless, without will. I didn't think I could stand one more test.

How do you decide to tear down the castle you've worked so hard to build? How do you say goodbye to a 20-year relationship, to a whole life? It wasn't just me, there were four other people involved and the decision would affect us all forever. And I had to make it? It wasn't fair.

I had played all my cards. I had run out of ideas. I had tried all the alternatives. I had knocked on every door... and nothing.

I had been on psychiatric medication for over six months now to control anxiety attacks. Every night I had to change my nightclothes and sometimes my bed sheets because of the amount of sweat I produced during sleep.

I had forgotten what it felt to be happy, really happy. We were seven years into this carnival; 2,555 days of uncertainty. Where was I going to get the courage to ask him to leave? At that time, it was a matter of survival. We had three daughters! They needed at least one of their fathers to be sane and stand up for them. That has been one of the most painful moments I have had to go through. One that I put off for five years. It took too much courage. I asked for advice from everyone who crossed my path.

I asked everyone for permission to make a life-or-death decision. The uncertainty I lived through those years led me to that state of self-destruction and burnout.

And how could we have imagined that one decision would have so many consequences? As a couple we gambled everything to, in our understanding as entrepreneurs, build a firm and stable heritage for our family.

A business option that seemed to be a dream come true. We put everything into it, resources, time, heart and enthusiasm. And nothing went as we had imagined. One stumble after another, one obstacle after another. Until we went bankrupt.

In the hope of getting the boat afloat again, we ended up selling everything we owned, everything we had at hand. Because the dream was big, there was no chance of giving up.

But no, it did not come to fruition. We lost everything, with a 2-year-old daughter and another one on the way. From then on it was all downhill. And a terrible depression followed. Months and months with our faces to the ground, both of us crying our eyes out.

This depression caused my daughters' father to develop a more serious disorder. His brain stopped producing certain substances, until one day, he began to show evidence of a bipolar disorder that eventually developed into a more serious one with features of schizophrenia and psychotic outbreaks.

In this process, he was in and out of the Mental Health Institute several times. Sometimes for a week and sometimes for more than a month. This was necessary to stabilize him and return him to a state of sanity. I don't even want to tell you about the situations we lived through that made it unavoidable to put him in the hands of professionals.

The medicines I needed to buy for him were very expensive and there was no way he could avoid taking them, so all my

work efforts were focused on getting the money to pay for them month after month. There was almost nothing left to pay for the rest.

How could I imagine that this reality was possible in those happy days when we dedicated ourselves to traveling, living a good life? Where our biggest concern was what new car model we were going to buy that year. When we dreamed of starting our family, having happy little blond children. We were only able to see ourselves in that Liverpool ad picture of "The Happy Family".

Some years later, in an apparent period of stability, it happened that, after many, many months of sexual abstinence, there was an encounter, a single intimate contact. And against all odds, a few weeks later I discovered that I was pregnant.

Madness! you will say. And yes... absolute crazy moment. That when she was born, nine months later, it brought us the surprise that we had a new daughter with a particular genetic condition.

She had Down Syndrome. Accompanied by one of the common traits of this syndrome, a cardiopathy (malformation of the heart) that required prompt intervention if we wanted her to live more than a year.

With no health insurance, no job, no savings and nowhere to draw on for resources, we began the adventure of seeking how we were going to get her through open heart surgery. A nightmare that, of course, I did not want or need to live, in the midst of everything I have already told you.

Facing again the possibility of the death of a child was not in my plans, so I used my last economic, mental and energetic resources to try to save her from that prognosis.

In order for you to understand the context, I will go back a little further. To tell you how this group of growth experiences started.

My greatest longing has always been to be a mother. Since I married very young and didn't want to tie myself to the care of a child from the age of 22, we decided to wait and live our life as a couple. In those wonderful years we were able to travel the world. Do whatever we wanted. Go out, stay up late, live life as we were single. Those were good years.

When it was time to have a child, things started to get complicated. It was the first time I realized that you have no control over almost anything. You may want to be a mom or dad, but life may have other plans for you. So, we started trying for three months and nothing. At six, we started to get impatient. After a year, that was a tragedy.

We went through multiple treatments, monitoring, hormones, etc. Until, after two and a half years, I managed to get pregnant. The joy, happiness and fulfillment I felt at that moment was unparalleled. In fact, I thought that once I had my baby in my arms, everything would finally be all right.

I lived a pregnancy full of love and care. I dreamed of a life full of moments by his side. I imagined his little face and

what he would smell like. I felt a love that grew with every heartbeat. We all looked forward to him. He was a boy, the family's firstborn.

So, it took us a long time to choose his name. We would name him Christopher.

It happened that, eight months into my pregnancy, I started having contractions, lots of them. We went to see my doctor, who checked me carefully. On the ultrasound my baby's heart wasn´t audible anymore.

- This isn't right," he said in alarm, "I can't hear it anymore!
- What? You're kidding, right? -I answered with some hesitation.
- No, it's not," the doctor answered. I don't understand what happened, everything was perfect.

His heart had stopped inside me. And with it, time stopped. Like a lump of sugar, all the dreams I had dissolved. A moment when I found it hard to breathe, to think.

What was I going to do with all my days from then on? What was it all about?

I won't go into detail about the process that followed that moment, but it was very long, very painful and it became my first big test to go through. The first time I actually experienced not having control over anything and learned that there are things I must accept, even if I feel like dying.

After having lived through that experience, it was terrifying to even think about the possibility that this daughter of mine, my special girl, could meet the same fate.

Are you starting to get a picture of what I was going through in that year of the Apocalypse?

You may ask... And how do you get out of something like that? Where do you start?

For many years I became this horror story. It was all I thought about, all I talked about. I became the perfect victim. And how could I not be? Life had been so mean to me. I suddenly felt that everything I had done was wrong. That no matter how hard I tried, things always went against me. That I had the worst luck! I visualized myself as the cartoon character who, wherever he goes, has a rainy gray cloud raining on top of his head.

I told you that both he and I cried a river. Mine is no joke. I cried every day for many years. I could no longer conceive of my days without a moment to cry, to unburden myself. I felt such a deep sadness, there were not enough tears to wash it away. The problem was this became a habit and being sad was part of my personality.

In my basic shopping, boxes of tissues were always included, because I used them so much.

The good news I have for you are the same that someone gave me one day... Ready?

Every step you have taken throughout your life has brought you to this point where you are. You have got to this moment because of a combination of decisions you made without being forced by anyone.

What? You mean I chose for my first child not to be born alive? For my business to go bankrupt? For my husband to lose his mind? For my daughter to be born with Down Syndrome?

If you close your eyes and from the depths of your heart,

you remember the journey that has led you to this moment,

every event, every time you have made a decision, every time you have chosen your attitudes and your ways of dealing with situations, you will realize that on every occasion you considered options to choose and you chose.

Right? Wrong? The reality is that it no longer matters. It was the best you could have chosen at that moment, from the place you were in, with the conscience you had, considering the elements you had in front of you, how you felt, etc.

We all have the deepest reasons for being the way we are and doing what we do.

The first step I had to take, the very first step, was to become aware of this. To take responsibility for myself, for my decisions, for what I thought, for what I ate (which by the way I ate very little because I was always depressed); for what I drank, for what I allowed to enter through my ears, for what I saw or decided to stop seeing.

Taking 100% responsibility for oneself is not an easy task. It involves, in the first instance, forgiving yourself for everything that makes you feel guilty. For everything you think you have done wrong. For the harm you think you have caused to others or that you have actually caused them.

The exercise I had to do to become aware, assimilate and accept that I was the creator of my own destiny was the most difficult process I have ever had to go through. I realized that I loved myself very little. All these events had

made me forget about myself almost completely. I had placed myself as the last in line. I did nothing for myself or for my welfare. I did nothing to make me happy and to encourage me. I had distanced myself from everything and everyone. I had no friends, no social life. And the most important thing I realized was that for many years I had been swept along by the current. I was like a weathervane at the wind´s mercy. I realized I had stopped fighting.

That was the saddest moment of all. It was heartbreaking to realize that I had "failed" myself the most. Looking in the mirror and realizing the emptiness reflected in my eyes.

Does it resonate with you? Have you lived or are you living a similar moment to this one?

I imagine it is like when a person who was in a coma for many months, reopens his eyes and realizes everything that happened while he was asleep. Of all the events he missed, of how much the people around him, his family, his friends, have changed.

Re-opening your eyes to life. Discovering your reality. Connecting with your Self can be overwhelming and scary. It is the first mandatory step to begin your process of recovery and reunion with yourself.

Throughout these pages, I will tell you in detail what my process was. How I was able to jump from those moments of tragedy, despair and sadness to the woman I am today. To this strengthened and happy woman. I will tell you how I became a Valkyrie, a Bulletproof Woman and what this means.

But most importantly, and the reason I am sitting here today writing these letters, is because I want to give you a road map. Crossing this road, for you, doesn't have to be as hard as it was for me. There are countless ways to live life and there are countless tools and paths available to you to make this journey. And... you are not alone.

Which path do you choose this time?

Chapter 2 | Bulletproof Woman

Here comes Bulletproof Woman. Someone said, referring to me in a business meeting a few years ago. I had joined a Network Marketing company months ago. To begin to succeed, I had to work hard on my personal growth and my confidence in speaking and interacting with strangers.

As I listened to him, I opened my eyes wide in surprise. In that instant, the movie of my life flashed through my head. And like in a superhero story, I visualized how each event, each experience, each challenge, had been creating layers on my being. I visualized how my heart and my stomach had been lined with different types of metals that made them strong and resistant: aluminum, brass, copper, silver, gold, platinum. Each metal in order of strength. And at that moment I could feel as if I was actually lined with an armor that made me invincible.

I have heard several times that success is full of failure stories. That those who are able to get up again from a fall, once and a thousand times, are the ones who can really feel fulfillment in their lives.

And if you don't learn to enjoy the road you need to travel to reach a goal, you are missing out on the best part. As Joan Manuel Serrat's beautiful song says: **You build the road by walking through it.**

You choose whether the road is a great daily adventure or an ordeal to be endured. The decision belongs to no one but you.

Nietzsche's oft-repeated phrase: **What doesn't kill you makes you stronger**, made perfect sense to me at that moment. I understood that, without knowing how, I felt powerful, capable, in a word: Resilient. I realized how much I had transformed myself through all those years of trials and unfortunate events.

I must confess I was fascinated by the new title I had been given. I felt so identified that I adopted it as my own, I made it my identity.

For the first time I became aware of all my courage. I realized how much love I had been able to feel in order to resist through the days when I was terrified of a new day. How I was able to overcome adversity like a cat on its back, for love. Out of love for my daughters' father, out of love for them, out of love for life.

I understood how a Bulletproof Woman is made up. We are women who are always on the lookout for everything and everyone. We are busy covering all the flanks. Worldwide known as "multitaskers". Women who choose to wave the flag of awareness, wellness and mental, physical, emotional and spiritual health.

We have a great interest in being well trained, surrounded by tools that make our lives more pleasant and functional. Women committed to constant growth to improve the version of themselves, every day. That we have decided to HEAL.

I have a special affection and admiration for Robin Sharma, speaker and author of important books that have shaken

me many times and have taken me out of my comfort zone to throw myself into the arena. From him, I heard this phrase: **Those who exhaust themselves the most in training bleed the least in battle.**

At the beginning, I told you the idea of this book was born from the deepest and most genuine interest to share with you my story and some valuable tools, the ones that have been most meaningful to me. Today I have the firm belief that it is not necessary to learn the hard way, to have to suffer so much to find the way back to your Being.

If you make the committed decision to train yourself, to grow, to be brave and open the door that opens inward. To know yourself and gradually turn on the light in every dark corner that exists within you and that, until today have not allowed you to live happily and fully. If you accept the challenge of training yourself day by day, in acquiring hard and soft skills. I assure you that you will bleed less in battle. You will have many more resources to react better when life presents you with challenges. And believe me, there is not a single life story without challenges.

Therefore, I want to ask you to firmly believe that, if this book has reached your hands, if it caught your attention for some reason, if it was recommended to you or given to you as a gift, there is a reason. It is because, surely, something of what you read in these chapters will reflect you in some way.

I am so grateful that you allow me to be a mirror and that, through my stories, you can find common ground or similarities that will make you wake up, get out of the lethargy in which you may find your way back to yourself.

Today, I feel so proud of myself. So satisfied with what I've worked so hard to rebuild. And the most valuable thing of all that I have learned is, no matter how many times I fall or how many more times I have to build from scratch, I AM READY. Because my strength today is no longer outside of me. It goes with me wherever I go. I carry as an imprint in my Being "resilience", which I have been developing in all these years. I handle situations totally differently and stand from a different place.

The term "resilience" comes from the Latin *resilio*, which means to go back. It refers to the human being's capacity to face life's adversities. The way to get through and overcome destabilizing emotional painful events or traumas to which life exposes you.

This change involves a transformation within difficult situations to be able to adapt better and even positively.

This is one of the main pillars on which a Bulletproof Woman is based. You become a woman capable of facing adversity without fear and, with all your tools help, you can face any challenge.

New hard situations no longer bring you down, but you are able to take advantage of them and, on the contrary, they serve you as a lever to advance a little further on your path of growth. You become capable of transforming everything into something positive and constructive.

I can see now that I was lost for too many years. Immersed in a gray life of sadness and meaninglessness. Without direction. Lost in a day to day life that was consuming me and, without realizing it, I began to fade away.

For me, a gray life is the one lived by conformists, by people installed in victimization and complaint, in criticism and dismay, in isolation and disaffection. Mainly those who live in their own lack of love.

Today, that I have managed to recover my colors one by one and along the way I have also been able to color some of the lives of the people with whom I have had the fortune to cross. I know that there are many paths and, as I told you before, you have the possibility to choose. You choose from the moment you open your eyes. You make thousands of decisions every day without realizing it.

At a higher level of awareness, you are able to make better decisions. These can be more accurate and much less stumbling.
There is a popular saying which says **you don't know how strong you can be until being strong is the only option.**

If there is one thing I am sure of, it is right now, you don't know what you are capable of. Maybe because you haven't dared. Maybe because you're full of limiting, external, self-imposed beliefs. Maybe because you've never asked yourself the right questions.

Later on I will share with you the great pillars that support a Bulletproof Woman. And then, it will be your decision if you stay where you are or you start walking, really moving forward in pursuit of the life you always dreamed of living. If you bet on a happy and fulfilled life. And you are willing to learn all change begins with yourself.

I change, the world changes.

If you dare and you feel ready, the time is here...

Are you coming?

Chapter 3 | Your Limit

Human beings have great endurance. Our body, like a perfect machine, is designed to live 120 years optimally[1]. It has an incredible capacity, self-healing and return to balance because several systems interact with each other for you to recover. None of them could function on its own. The cardiovascular needs the nervous and respiratory systems, the muscular needs the skeletal, the digestive needs the digestive and the respiratory systems.

Your body acts as a whole, as a unit. If any of the organs begins to deteriorate or becomes ill, the rest of the body seeks to compensate for the failure by increasing or decreasing the production of substances of all kinds, to seek balance. And in almost all cases, it succeeds divinely. It functions again in its usual perfection.

The problem begins when, for some reason, the element that is causing the imbalance does not cease. When the invading, aggressor or toxic factor continues. This is when a disease manifests itself.

This image is perfect to describe what actually happens in a family nucleus. A family is conceived and designed to grow in harmony, based on love and support among each of its elements.

---

1 Angarita, Ana Marisol (2009). Designed to survive, BBC News Mundo. https://www.bbc.com

A family is the sustenance of an individual. That is why the "mission" that is entrusted to us from the moment we begin to grow, develop and start using our common sense is to look for the one with whom we will continue our journey, when we have completed our time within the primary group in which we were born. And so, we continue in an endless cycle.

But is this all life is about? Do you grow, reproduce, reproduce and die? Of course it is not. Your life, my life, is full of color scales and we come to this planet to be happy, to fulfill ourselves and to evolve, as individuals, as a human race.

Well, going a little bit out of the theoretical. I am going to talk to you from my experience. Today I am a woman, in my forties. I could say I think I have reached an age where I am full of experiences, and I still have a lot of life ahead of me. The family reality that I live today is nothing like what I had projected at some point. I am no longer conflicted about getting out of that endless cycle (like in the Disney´s Lion King movie).

You will realize throughout these pages I am a lover of sayings and famous quotes. I believe they contain a great deal of wisdom derived from the experiences of others. But let's not get sidetracked. I was telling you about a saying: Do you want to make God laugh? Tell him your plans.

My experience has taught me you can only imagine or create in your mind, a road map that, from who you are and what you know at that moment, you believe will lead you to your goals. The goals you have at that moment. And you almost always do your best to achieve them.

It has also taught me that, although your mind makes you believe that you control situations, the reality is that you can only control your reaction to what appears, but everything outside of you, has its own course, its own ways of reacting and developing.

I am telling you about my reality which, as I described you in the human body's process, when one of the pillars of my family, my husband, started to not be well, I tried to compensate the situation with more care and dedication. I thought it was easy. That since I was a loving, dedicated, focused and persevering person, it was a matter of time before everything would go back to the way it was.

I never calculated, anticipated or imagined the size of the mess we were getting into. Today I can tell you, with all certainty, if in those years I had had the level of awareness and attention that I have now, I would have realized, first, that the situation we had reached after the economic meltdown was far from being solved. In all likelihood I would also have been able to focus on the most important thing: **ME.**

There was too much going on at once. I got my hands full of problems for many years. After he got sick, I had neither the capacity nor the head to put out the little fires that constantly needed to be solved. It was just too much. I had two small daughters, a sick husband, who could not go back to work. No savings, no assets. I lived far from my family, so it was difficult for them to help me.

And inside that reality, in the blink of an eye, nine years passed, nine! Now that I think about it, it seems like an eternity. During all of them, my capacity only gave me enough to survive the thousand and one challenging, distressing and strange situations that were happening to me.

And I got used to it. I got used to living in anguish, to being depressed, to living away from my family and friends (the few that remained after the mental illness manifested itself). Day after day passed, week after week and nothing seemed to change, move or modify. Without realizing it, I was in a downward spiral.

Many of my mornings, just as I woke up, when everything was still quiet, I would open my eyes, take a deep breath and wonder how long it would take for this to end.

Living in this state of constant uncertainty for that many years destroys anyone. Remaining in a reality that does not change and at the same time does not offer us security or allow us to have moments of peace, can bring other kinds of important consequences.

The important note here is, what should you do about it? Do you leave everything and everyone and go in search of a new reality that is not so complex and overwhelming? No, it's not that easy. There are many elements involved. In most cases: children, shared lives long histories, but, above all, lots of dreams.

As long as things don't get really serious, we humans get used to it, we live at the mercy of events. Another quote refers that **you get used to everything except not eating.**

So, what happens when you begin to die a little every day, without realizing it? When your eyes lose their shine. When you look at yourself in the mirror in the morning and wrinkles start to appear on your face sooner and sooner. When it is no longer so easy to smile. When your head does not stop spinning day and night, asking you a thousand questions.

Now, I ask you: What is really serious? This also varies from person to person. What is intolerable for some is not so important for others. This depends on who you are, how you were raised, your beliefs and values, but, above all, your self-concept. What may seem normal to me may be a tragedy for someone else.

At that time, it used to happen that a friend of mine, with a small child, would come to me crying because her baby had a fever. I would just stare at her in disbelief that this seemed so serious, after all I had been through.

But for her, that reality was the most overwhelming thing that had ever happened and that was not wrong, it was just the way it was.

A woman who loves herself, who has high self-esteem, who is capable of taking her rightful place in any situation, allows much less things than those who are culturally used to be the last in line, sacrificing herself for everyone, "putting up with it" because she believes that is her role.

In my case it was a brief, but transcendent moment of divine enlightenment that made me realize that my situation was not going to change. It would not change a bit if change did not come from me. I´ve waited too many years for things to change outside.

That moment of light made me see how destroyed I really was. That I felt like an old woman. I had no strength, no spirit at all. My eyes were always lost. I would stare at a point and spend hours like that. But, above all, I felt sick, unbalanced. I was falling into the same abyss as he was.

Right in the middle of this moment of awareness, I looked my daughter's eyes and all I found was sadness. I don't know how, but that was the trigger for me to decide. I realized that, if I didn't leave their father, something very bad was going to happen to us and it would be very soon. So, I started to move in different direction. I realized that, as in the analogy I made at the beginning with the human body, in this one, the sick organ was making the rest of the body sick too, it was impossible to restore its balance.

And you, with how many unfulfilling situations that do not make you happy, have you been satisfied throughout your life? I am sure with more than one.

Have you ever really sat down and analyzed this deeply? When you look in the mirror, what do you see?

How is your energy level? Do you wake up happy and eager to start your day?

How many sacrifices are you willing to make for an "ideal"? Has this "ideal" been created and conceived by you or is it someone else's expectation?

Let's do a committed analysis exercise of the reality you live today and what is your driving force? What is your motive? On average, how many days of the week do you do activities that fulfill you? What are you passionate about doing? The kind of activity where there is no time or space because it connects you to who you are. Where do you place yourself right now? Are you your main priority?

In some paragraphs I have shared with you so far, I commented the purpose of this book, which is, in some way, to put a mirror in front of you so you can look at yourself. That you can become aware of where are you standing.

I do not intend to incite you to follow my steps, but I do want to make you see everything in this life has a remedy, even the most tangled and complex moments. Maybe the remedy is not the one you would be expecting, but there is one.

There is always a light at the end of the road and even the darkest night has a dawn.

I want to make you see you don't need to be in a life or death situation to start walking towards a fulfilling and happy life. What is indispensable is for you know the first step is to begin to take responsibility for who you are, to be sincere in the matter of congruence, of what you do, of what you say, of what you think.

Your happiness does not depend on anyone **but yourself**. Taking responsibility for yourself implies having your observer element active and becoming aware of everything you do automatically, without really realizing what you do and say or why you do it or why you say it.

How many things do you do because that's how others do it? Or do you believe something because you were told it was so? From the simplest things like how to peel and cut a cucumber to your opinion on homosexuality. You will realize that almost everything you do, you do by imitation or because that's the way it is, without questioning yourself.

Are you where you are because you want to be or because that's the way it is? What is it that you really want, think, desire and would like to do?

Ask yourself, what is your limit to be able make that decision, the one that will make you feel free. I can't tell you what decision to make, but what I can share with you is: the solution to the problem, that master key that opens

the door to the clarity you long for, will not be found on the outside.

Most of the answers you need live inside you, you know them, but you are afraid to see them, to face them and to dare to take a different path than others expect from you.

The exit door opens inward.

And it is time to open it!

Chapter 4 | Hands on

Standing at that starting line, at ground zero, everything seemed to have large dimensions. I felt the size of an ant in front of Everest. The size of a challenge that was far beyond me.

Not only was I absolutely exhausted and drained on every level, but I had no idea where to start. I had finally made the terrifying decision and there was no turning back. It may sound cruel to say, but I felt like the shackle that had kept my leg bound for so long had been opened. I was free!

The big challenge now was what the hell to do with that freedom. I had no idea where to go or which path I should follow. I shared with you that heartbreaking moment when I realized how empty I felt and how sad it was to see that I no longer knew myself. I had lost my identity. I didn't remember what my favorite food was or my favorite music. I didn't know what kind of clothes I liked best.

It had been so long since I had bought something, anything for myself. That it hadn't provide to me any kind of pleasure. That I hadn't indulge myself, so I had to start there. By closing my eyes, taking a deep breath, and taking the first step to recognize myself again.

Although for a moment you may feel like you are all alone, the reality is that we are never alone. This wonderful universe is always looking out for us. We are surrounded by help and support. Tools that are available to us when we are ready to receive them. Even if you can't see them when you are immersed in your nightmares, they are present all the time.

When you are immersed in darkness you lose the ability to see the light, it doesn't mean it's not there, you just can't see it. When I was able to open a small crack, the light started to come in. I realized life was about so much more. That the world outside my cave had many colors. That there were happy people. That not everything was a tragedy.

I was fortunate to have a friend. She is the friend we all wish we had. The one who, without asking too many questions, is there 24 X 7, in case you decide to let her help you.
This great friend took care of me every step of the way, with lots of love and great amounts of patience and understanding. It was she who approached me to different types of therapies and professional help. The truth is that we tried everything: psychological, energetic, spiritual therapies, etc. I got something good out of all of them and I advanced a little each time.

Reality is every human being is different, we are armed in different ways and, therefore, not all of us need the same kind of help. What may be a universal panacea for me, may not be of use to some people at all. The important thing is to be open and receptive and let yourself be helped.

Asking for help is not bad, it is the first step to begin to heal. When you are in the midst of your overwhelm or sadness, you can hardly see clearly and make the best conscious decisions.

If you were to introspect on this issue now, what would you tell me? How do you feel in that area? Are you an approachable person? A teachable one?

In my experience when you are in the middle of the hurricane, it is very complex to see solutions. Everything looks black. Sometimes we need other eyes, another mind outside our reality to helps us see things with objectivity, without so many emotions. Opening up to help when we are wounded is a complex issue, but it is possible.

I want to share with you what was really a turning point in my life. This personal work demanded from me a serious commitment and permanence. I joined a Semiology of Everyday Life Consciousness Development Group. This inner work consisted of weekly meetings with a group of 15 people who, like me, needed to start knowing themselves. Each level consisted of 16 sessions and in the end, I took 5 levels. If you do numbers, there were 80 weeks. A total of 20 months in which I worked uninterruptedly on myself.

The first module was: *"Self-knowledge"*. At this stage I realized how angry I was with life and with everyone. I was living in my destructive thoughts. My internal conversation only talked about negative things. I was stuck in victimization and complaining. I realized how many hours a

day I spent absorbed in these destructive thoughts causing my perception of my life to be as destructive as they were. I was able to realize that I was creating my own depressing reality of scarcity. No one else was doing it for me.
You've probably heard that raising your level of consciousness is of utmost importance. But what does this mean?

In a simple way it means being able to be "here and now". It may sound simple, but it involves starting to let go of past grudges and anxieties about the future and placing ourselves only in the now, in what is happening in the present moment. And just as if you wake up from a coma, you open your eyes and realize that you have been absent from yourself for years. That your thoughts and beliefs have ruled your life and that much of what you do and decide is a function of this and not of who you really are and what you want.

Starting to take responsibility for yourself is not as simple as it sounds. It implies to stop blaming others for what happens to us and, of course, it is much more comfortable to blame others for the decisions that we have not dared to take and also for those that we did take and did not turn out as we wanted. Taking responsibility for how we feel, for our dissatisfaction, for everything that makes us unhappy but that we continue to do because we believe that this will make others happy. Sometimes you spend many years of your life pleasing everyone, looking for their approval, their recognition, because you only feel seen or valued if someone from the outside recognizes you as valuable.

This friend I was telling you about before, told me one day: If only you could see yourself with the eyes I see you.... I confess that, when I heard her, it was very tender. I did not understand the depth of her words. It was until I was able to see myself from the inside, from my Being, when I was able to eliminate my self-judgment and modified the concept I had of me and I was able to see myself with those same eyes with which she saw me from the beginning. When this happened, and even though so many years had passed, I couldn't help but call her and tell her: Today, I can see myself with the eyes you saw me with, and I don't like what I see. I love it!

You will read in several paragraphs how it was that I began to see life in color, and this is literal. It was as if I could breathe easier, without heaviness. When I could stand here and now and let go for a moment of the pain of the past and the anguish and uncertainty of the future. I was able to see the wonder of the present with the unlimited gifts it gives us. I was able to see the miracles that happen before our eyes every day and that, if we are absent from us, pass us by.

I want to share with you 6 basic keys that changed my reality in an important way at that moment and helped me to regain inner peace.

1. Practice silence, both in your speech and internally.

At first, this may be one of the biggest challenges you've ever faced. You will find that it takes practice. Gradually you will be able to slow down the torrent of thoughts running through your head. Most of them unconsciously.

One of the tools that helped me the most was to practice the "One Minute Meditation". You can use this technique at any time, even in the middle of the situation that is upsetting you, when you are angry, desperate or distressed and need to regain your peace. You can also use it if you have trouble sleeping.

It consists of the following:

Sit with both feet on the floor and place your hands on your lap, either with your palms facing up or down. It does not matter. Just check that they are placed in a symmetrical position.
Keep your back straight. Imagine that someone is pulling a string from just above the top of your head.
Gently close your eyes.
For the next 60 seconds just concentrate on your breathing. If you get distracted during this minute, it is normal. It does not mean you are doing it wrong. If you catch yourself doing this, just bring your attention back to your breathing. At the end of the time, open your eyes and observe yourself. You will notice that you feel different, a little more refreshed and relaxed. Perhaps a little more aware.

The more you practice this meditation, the better you will feel.

This simple step-by-step practice can change your perception of reality very quickly, and the best part is that the more you practice it, the more visible the results become. And with practice, that minute can be reduced to an instant and, with a deep breath closing your eyes, you can return to your center.

As I mentioned, this matter of becoming conscious, starting to be here and now, is a matter of developing the habit.

Another thing I did was to bring with me a little notebook in my bag, which I called "the crazy lady of the house" and every time I realized I was lost in negative or distressing thoughts, I would take out my notebook and put a stick with the pen in it. At the end of the day I would do a stick count. The first few days I was frightened by the number, but it gradually decreased as my moments of awareness increased.

2. Organize your activities

Never underestimate the value of order, especially mental order. One of the best decisions I was able to make was to become aware of my habits, good and bad. One of the ones I implemented was to start organizing myself. To not let the day just go by.

I bought a physical planner, one of those big ones where, at a glance, you can see the whole week. I started to write down in it the things I wanted to do during the following days. At the beginning, I realized that I had an absolute mess, in my meals, in my sleeping hours, that I didn't do any physical activity and, above all, that I had no activities that would increase my growth and my knowledge.

Then I scheduled my mealtimes, reading times and the activities I had with my daughters. This helped me to see where I was spending my days and my energy. I could see how many hours I was spending doing nothing, just getting caught up in my own destructive thoughts and worries.

Organizing your activities is the second step of consciousness that I recommend you to do. Don't live like the shrimp in the popular saying, the one that gets carried away by the current. Take control of your days little by little and as a result, with time, you will be able to take control of your life. But it starts with the first day.

It helps to take a look at your schedule at night before going to bed so that you can have peace and certainty about what the next day will bring. This way, your mind is programmed to do what you are telling it is important.

3. Don't take things personally

One of the great books that cannot be missing in your library, and you certainly need to read, if you have not already done so, is the work of Don Miguel Ruiz, "Los

Cuatro Acuerdos" (The Four Agreements). In it, the author writes:

There is no reason to suffer. The only reason you suffer is because you choose to. If you look at your life you will find many excuses for suffering, but no valid reason. The same applies to happiness. The only reason you are happy is because you choose to be happy. Happiness is a choice, as is suffering.

Not taking things personally is one of the four agreements described. It indicates that doing so is the ultimate expression of selfishness, since it implies the belief that everything revolves around us. It says if we choose to follow our heart without taking anything personally, even if we are in the midst of conflict, we will live happily with inner peace and remain in a state of bliss.

The greatest step of consciousness you will ever experience is to realize when you speak, you are only speaking about yourself. The same is true for every person you meet and encounter. What a person says and thinks only speaks of who they are and how they think, it has nothing to do with who you are and think. Therefore, it has nothing to do with you and has no reason to affect you.

One of the big questions I was taught to ask myself in these Consciousness Development Groups I told you about, when I made a judgment or assertion was:
What does that tell you about yourself?

Ahhhhhh! (expression of despair). Asking me this question, on every occasion, was like a bucket of cold water in my head. Little by little I became aware that everything I said only spoke about me and what I had to work on much harder.

What I see in you, I work on in me. What you hate only speaks about you. These are two ways of saying that only you can and should take care of yourself. That you are only responsible for how you react to situations and not about the situations themselves. If you become aware of this, little by little you will become a much less conflictive person. You will learn to flow with the things that come up in a subtle and graceful way.

4. Avoid complaining

Dr. Alfonso Ruiz Soto, creator of Semiology of Everyday Life coined this forceful phrase: **Complaint is the expression of the lack of ability to resolve a conflict in my reality. It only shows the lack of commitment with my own Self because it reflects the ignorance I have about my Being.**

The first time I read this definition of complaint, I felt ashamed of myself. For realizing that, for years, I had done nothing but complain and victimize myself. I blamed everything on the outside for how I felt on the inside. And as these lines say, I realized that I was only reflecting the deep ignorance I had about myself. I was constantly denoting my lack of resolve.

Just as I did with my negative thoughts, I began to keep a written record of the number of complaints that came out of my mouth during the day. Not counting all the ones I thought. The result was very embarrassing. I will only say that the notebook ran out of pages too soon.

Complaining is the manifestation of HOW NOT TO. It is the pessimistic view of everything that happens. And how can you change it? By starting to put your focus and attention on the HOW TO. And this is achieved through gratitude. Every day is a gift, not an entitlement. Whatever appears in your life is designed just for you, tailored for you, for your growth and evolution, that's how perfect the universe is. Therefore, gratitude is to flow with what appears and receive what is given to you with open arms.

I have another friend who is very dear to me, who has conducted scientific studies on how gratitude is capable of not only transforming your reality into a better one, but of changing the course of chronic degenerative diseases, even modifying your genetic information. That is how powerful positivism is VS negativity.

Complaining makes you sick, gratefulness heals. And it is up to you to decide which one to focus on.

5. Believe in yourself, even if others do not.

It seems simple, doesn't it? Well, it's not simple at all. At least, it wasn't for me. Believing in myself again has been the hardest job I have ever had to do. Regaining your self-esteem is no easy task. Especially when you've been the focus of so many years of being the focus of stigma, of alienation from your social groups, your groups of friends and your family. When you have so many failed attempts. When the dream of your life succumbed to adversity. When you feel that you have failed everything and everyone, mainly yourself.

The first step is FORGIVENESS. To accept, in all cases, you did the best you could from the person you were at the time, from the knowledge and level of awareness you had. And that, like you, everyone around you also did the best they could from their level of understanding and awareness. If they could have, they would have done better. And be thankful that today, you can do better than yesterday. Every day is an opportunity to be a better version of yourself. Today you can choose to act differently. You can choose to raise your awareness level and as a result, make better decisions.

Gradually you realize needing external approval to feel happy and complete, over time, leads to frustration, pain and disappointment. Because your life is based on expectations of how others will act. Disappointments are nothing more than expectations that were not met.

We tend to confuse dreams, faith and goals with expectations. The difference is expectations are an abstract reality created by you that actually DO NOT EXIST and are based on what you expect from someone else. As you may have noticed, almost every time, things do not turn out as you expected or as you envisioned them. Reality is you have no control over how people react. This is why expectations necessarily lead to disappointment. Therefore, if you don't want to be disappointed, avoid having them.

The key is to transform expectations based on others, by what YOU expect to achieve and how YOU expect to act. Build your own goals and dreams along the way. Write your own road map.

As for me, as I progressed, I realized I had the ability to provide myself with everything I needed and had demanded so much from others:

Can you imagine not needing something external to feel full, satisfied, complete and happy? Well, the good news is that it is perfectly possible. All that you are looking for is already within you, it is intrinsic to your Being, you just have to open your eyes to see it and have an open mind. The answer is already there, you just have to be ready to listen to it.

6. Review your priorities

I want you to answer these questions honestly honesty:

- Where do you rank on your list of priorities?
- What activities do you do during the day that give you satisfaction and contentment?
- What are you passionate about?
- What is most important to you today?
- How do you take care of your health, mentally, spiritually and physically?
- How is your nutrition (the quality of what you eat and drink)?

These are questions just for you. Once you have answered them, I want to ask you to do the exercise of reordering your priorities. Dare to put yourself first in line. I want to ask you to schedule, in an agenda, activities during your week just for you. That fill your soul, that make you happy.

I am going to share an analogy. If you visualize yourself as a jug of water, you will know that in order to fill the glasses of others, you need to be full. If your pitcher is empty, what can you give to others?

In my current life, I am a single mother of three daughters, and one is a little girl with special needs. The demands for love, time, money and effort are many. And I have only been able to play a good role as a mom, friend, counselor, psychologist, doctor, etc., since I work on myself and provide moments of richness and personal growth.

Love is not given, it is. YOU ARE LOVE! And true love is born from an inexhaustible source, it never ends and there is enough to give and give away. That love is within you, not outside. And if you manage to start by putting into practice these six guidelines that I have shared with you so far, you will be able to get in touch, for much longer, with the source. Therefore, your pitcher will be full so that you can fill everyone else's glasses.

Here it is like in AA groups, one day at a time. Once you have answered them, I want to ask you to do the exercise of reordering your priorities. Dare to put yourself first in line. I want to ask you to schedule, in an agenda, activities during your week that are just for you. That fill your soul, that make you happy.

Cultivate your own powers, study and become wiser, more skillful and always act with respect for yourself. Work on being a determined person. Willpower is the unchanging purpose to carry a task, which you yourself decided to carry out, to its completion. Persistence is the secret to making your desires come true. It takes guts to achieve Glory.

WORK ON BEING A DETERMINED PERSON!

Chapter 5 | Responsibility

I want to share a concept with you: Reality is one and your life is the perception of that reality, from who you are.
One of the laws, found in the book of Kybalion, which is a document that describes the 7 universal laws upon which all creation rests:

As within is without and as without is within.

This means that whatever you are living on the outside is a reflection of how you see life and can therefore be changed. To begin to change anything, you have to change it yourself, inside you.

For more years than I would like to admit, I lived at the mercy of circumstances, prey to uncertainty, full of unfulfilled expectations. Frustrated. Sad. Unfulfilled. I lived in complaining and blaming others for everything that I was not capable of assuming.

Taking charge of your life means taking responsibility. Is it easy? No, it is not easy. We are full of fears, limiting beliefs, attachments, codependences, many of them inherited and many of these beliefs, we are not even aware of them, we just act automatically. While you were growing up all these beliefs were implanted in you without you realizing it and most probably without the one who implanted them in you being aware of them either.

One of the most vivid memories I have is a conversation I had with a nun of the Capuchin order, Mother Esperanza. She was very close to us during the most difficult years of my husband's illness. We loved her so much that we choose her as my little daughter's godmother. She represented her name, in all its splendor. Having her close to us filled us with hope, because she transmitted a lot of peace and a big light. She was an enormous support for me in so many days of anguish and uncertainty.

One day when we were gathered at my house and my heart shrank with sadness, seeing that things had lost their meaning. That I was only concerned with surviving, with enduring, with solving the problems the day presented, I sat down next to her and leaned my head on her shoulder.

- Mother, I said, do you think he will ever heal; do you think this is all just a bad dream and our life will go back to what it was before?

With her round little face, with a tender compassionate smile, she told me: "No my child, this illness is here to teach you something, something very important. It is the result of many errors of judgment and decision that, at the beginning, did not seem to have consequences. You have to accept that you, too, are partly responsible.

For too long you lived absent from what was important, certainly with priorities arranged in a way that did not benefit everyone involved. Perhaps out of selfishness and unconsciousness, and this is the result.

Every step you and he have taken, individually and together, the small and big decisions, have brought you to this moment. If you want something to change, you need to accept and take your share of responsibility in the first place.

I will never forget those wise words which, of course, left me speechless, not knowing how to respond. They marked the beginning of a change in my way of seeing and understanding what I was living. That night I stayed awake. Staring at the ceiling of my room. Minute by minute, ideas began to fall into place. As we say in Mexico: The coin finally fell.

This expression: The coin finally fell, has an origin that is worth telling you about. Until not too many years from now, before the cel phone´s era, city's public telephones worked with coins. In fact, if you look closely, even now you can still be fortunate enough to come across one. You would put the twenty-cent coin through the slot, dial the number you wanted to reach, and when they answered on the other end, then the twenty would drop into the inner box of the machine. If no one answered, you could press a button and the coin was returned to you.

The coin finally fell, means you manage to establish communication with your inner self. Your mind lights up and you understand. These moments are usually accompanied by a deep sigh and a surprised expression in the eyes. Later I also came to know them as aha moments. Moments when you finally understand and say:

Aha! As an expression that the point has become clear to you.

But one thing is to understand, another is to assume and the most difficult of all is to decide what you are going to do to act differently. To begin to take responsibility for your life and your decisions until you achieve 100%. To get to that point, you need to modify well-established life structures. You have to take risks. You have to face your primal fears. And by primary fears, I mean those that arise from within your body. Information that you have imprinted on it since you were a child and that makes you react in one way or another to the things that appear, automatically. The fear of being abandoned, of being cold, hungry, feeling unprotected. All the unconscious fears.

Today I know we can learn and change from a state of pain and suffering and evolve into one of happiness and inspiration. But reality is, (and I am sorry to have to tell you this) as long as you remain the same as always, as long as your actions remain the same, you cannot expect to obtain a new result or create a different reality.

Let's make a reflection to identify if your day-to-day life is based on resentment or on gratitude:

The first thing you need to know, if you have not heard it before from countless authors who teach, through their books, the importance of living here and now and how your mind is able to create your reality through your thoughts, is that **where your attention is, there is your energy.**

It is possible to abound on this subject in books by Eckhart Tolle, Napoleon Hill, T. Harv Ecker, Robin Sharma, Joe Dispenza, to name a few.

Each of these books has helped me to become aware of the importance of making this practice a daily routine to significantly change your life and be able to live in abundance and prosperity.

What do you focus your attention on? If you do it in love, then the fruit of that love is gratitude. Ask yourself: Is gratitude my main feeling during the day? To whom do you express your love? To your partner, to your children, to your boss (if you have one), to your government, to God.

Now, if what you express predominantly is criticism, the fruit you will get is resentment. Ask yourself in all honesty: Are resentments my main feelings? Is this how I feel?
Who or what are you criticizing? Your spouse, your children, your boss, your government, yourself, God?.

Do you criticize and complain about trivial things? Traffic, the price of things, long lines, physical appearance of others, others' actions.

If you are totally honest with yourself and take responsibility for what you think, say and do, you will realize, if you are very critical, the fruit of this criticism is resentment, accompanied by a persistent feeling of low-grade anger, that is, you give yourself small doses of poison that do not kill you, but keep you a little sick.

Have you ever thought about how many moments of your day you are actually happy, at peace and in a state of fulfillment? This state that keeps you a bit annoyed by so many things that happen at every moment can, in short, keep you in a state of permanent dissatisfaction and irritability without you even realizing it. And what you project outwardly is only the fruit of this.

So, what is the result? Do you express love or criticism? Is the taste sweet or bitter?

If the taste you have now is bitter, it is time for you to take that responsibility and change. Only you have the possibility to change, see and do things differently. If you consciously work on transforming your thoughts and feelings into positive, constructive and grateful ones, you will begin to visualize your life as prosperous and abundant, instead of frustrating and limited.

I remind you of the universal law quoted above:

As within, so without, and as without, so within.

My life needed a change. I needed to reinvent myself. It was already clear to me that nothing would change on the outside if I did not start making decisions. So, full of uncertainty and fear for everything that could happen, I started to take responsibility for myself as if my life depended on it, and in fact it did.

I am not talking about responsibility as such, because for many years I took responsibility for my house, for my family, for covering all the expenses we had the best I could. Of course, I did my best and did not hesitate to do what I had to do at that moment.

One of the attitudes I had, and I realized later on was, when it came to others, to help, to save, to satisfy the needs of others, there was no one better than me. I was always capable of risking anything, even my life if someone needed me. I named it the Wonder Woman Syndrome.

The problem was, when it came to me, I felt small, helpless, incapable of achieving even the smallest thing. I didn't believe I was enough to want, long for or desire anything for myself.

I had to work deeply, and still do, on this feeling of not being enough. One thing that helped me a lot was to think of myself as if I were someone else, just like that. I thought: if my friend needed this, or my daughter asked me for this, what would I do? And then it was much easier to start acting on my behalf.

I go back to what I was telling you. In a moment of clarity, I realized, although I was responsible for everything and everyone, I had not paid any attention or interest in my own well-being and especially in that of my daughters. I provided for them, house, food and the basic things they needed, but I had neglected to take care of their hearts, their joy and to make them feel happy and secure. And how could I do that if I myself felt disheartened, sad and insecure all the time.

Children are an extension of their parents. You want to know someone? Take a look at what their children are like. Their behavior shows a lot about what they experience at home. How they are treated. Whether they feel loved or are angry with life. They evidence beyond appearances.

And as in the example I gave you of the water pitcher, I couldn't fill their glasses with all the good stuff if my pitcher was empty. Today I can clearly see that what most impelled me to make the decision to separate from their dad, was the longing to see them happy again and to be able to repair all the damage that the situation had caused in them in a very evident way.

So, like in a poker game, I bet all the chips I had left. I bet on myself, on them and today, after eight years, I can assure you that I was not wrong. Today we are four united, happy, self-confident women, with a lot of things to work on, that's for sure. But we are no longer mortally wounded, we have been healing little by little.

I want to invite you to make a serious and committed introspection at this moment or at some point today. Remember I asked you the question: where do you place yourself in the queue of your priorities?
I would like to ask you other questions:

From 1 to 100, what is the percentage in which you place yourself in terms of taking responsibility for your well-being and your happiness?

What aspects of your life have you neglected? Those that are important to you.

If you have children, how do you perceive them? Do you see them happy, full and fulfilled? Do you notice them calm or are they angry with life? (at this point, it is obvious to consider that there are different behaviors specific to each age they live, such as adolescence).

Imagine for a moment they are your clearest mirror. What you see in them is a reflection of what you show.

Now I ask you to become aware for a moment of how you perceive the people you live with the most. What do you see? Do you observe happy and fulfilled people? Or only people who complain ç as soon as they open their eyes? What you see shows you your perspective on life.
What change would you need to start considering?

In future chapters we're going to talk about how you can make small and big changes without them having to be as radical or painful as they were for me. Or maybe some of the necessary changes will be painful, but necessary.

My ultimate goal will be for you to find peace and fulfillment.

Chapter 6 | Purpose

Living without a purpose is the same as wanting to sail the sea without a compass, without a road map, without knowing where you are going. It is important that your life has meaning so that you are not at the mercy of circumstances, like a ship without a rudder.

In my process of growth and reencounter with my essence, my heart and my why, there was an instant of light. It was as if something hit my head and opened my eyes to something that was always there but that because I had so many mental and emotional spiderwebs, I had not been able to see.

No woman should have to feel and experience all that I experienced and felt. For some reason I had chosen to walk the most paved road. The most winding. The fullest of obstacles. And this led me to grow up the hard way. But no matter why it happened that way, it had already happened and it was time to change course. To change lanes and start building a life with purpose. A life that would add to the lives of other women. I found **the reason** for all my suffering.

In the same way a body trains to perform in some discipline of exercise, day after day, strengthening the muscles little by little, improving times, increasing capacities, evolving into a better one; in the same way we strengthen our capacity for resilience, understanding and acceptance. We strengthen our spirit.

Undoubtedly, my graduation in resilience was facing my youngest daughter's genetic condition. During the 9 months of pregnancy, as every mother who has a life brewing inside her does, I visualized her little face, what she would look like, what her tone of voice would be, the color of her eyes, the temperature of her skin.

We had the name in mind from the beginning, she would be named Natalie. And a few weeks before she was born, my sister suggested to me: "Why don't you name her Lucia? The name fascinated me and made perfect sense, she had a Lucia vibe and that's what we named her. The scheduled date for her birth was December 13, the day Saint Lucia is celebrated. Coincidence? I don't think so.

Due to complications, the delivery date was moved forward four days. When I finally heard her cry in the operating room, I took a deep gratitude breath for her life.

In the distance I heard the doctor send for my husband.
-I want to show you something," he said. Your daughter looks very healthy, but we noticed that she has some physical features typical of Down syndrome. We can't know for sure until we do a karyotype test.

The karyotype is an individual set of chromosomes. Human beings have 46 chromosomes (23 pairs). One of these pairs is the one that differentiates the sexes (male XY and female XX). Chromosomes contain all genetic information of an individual, therefore, the karyotype is nothing more than the way in which this information is organized and arranged. We need to know if your daughter has Trisomy 21, that is, in the 21st pair she has three chromosomes instead of two.

And what does that mean? I thought in absolute ignorance on the subject. A few minutes later, they both approached me, I was still numb and confused from the anesthesia, and shared the news with me.

Showing a big a smile, and looking into my eyes with affection, the doctor told me: You are going to become a great family, it won't be easy, but you will make it. From that moment on we lived an internal storm. What was that? How could we manage this new challenge?

When they finally brought my daughter to my room and I looked at her, she was beautiful, but she was nothing like the one I had visualized for the previous nine months. She was quite different. She had features I had never seen before. Crinkly eyes. Ears like unopened flowers and she was all floppy, like she was made of plasticine. Nothing like the babies I knew.

And the pilgrimage began. For the first 30 days I did nothing but read and documented myself about Down Syndrome because, although I thought I knew about it, the reality was that I didn't have the faintest idea of anything. I read through tears. Tears of gratitude for her life, but also of frustration, fear, uncertainty, and regret.

Most of my fears were related to ignorance. I knew that when I found out what it was all about. I researched everything from what the genetic condition consisted of to the geriatric issues of people with this condition. This ultimately brought me a lot of peace and I realized that it was much less complicated than I had imagined in my stormy mind.

A little later, when she was two months, the pediatrician told us Lucia had a heart defect called ventricular septal defect.

When I received that news, my whole world fell apart. She had to go into surgery, and soon, if we wanted to keep her with us. The small detail was, if you remember what I told you earlier, we had no job, no savings and no health insurance, social security, or anything like that.

My God! What are we going to do? How am I going to be able to afford heart surgery? By then I had accumulated debts of several thousand.

Faced with this new circumstance, Down Syndrome was the least of it, that detail was unimportant, I just wanted him to live, I just wanted us to be able to meet this new challenge.

We don't know how brave we can be until being brave is the only option. Do you remember I shared, if it was for others, I could do anything? Especially if it was for my daughter. I decided to ask for help, there was no way I could handle such a challenge. there was no way I could handle a challenge of that size alone.

I opened a bank account and posted a call for help on social media: "I have a special daughter. She was born with Down Syndrome, has a heart condition and needs surgery". From the bottom of my heart, I ask for help with whatever you want and can share with me. Any help is immensely appreciated. My account number is...

And the miracle began. Little by little and a lot of people, friends, acquaintances, and strangers who contributed a little each one.

Thanks to the help of so many people, I was able to pay for all Lucía's support during the first year of her life, including all the therapies I had to take her to. It was a huge blessing.

Five months later, I took her to the Cardiology Institute in Mexico City to ask for a second opinion from the best country´s specialists and after the studies were done, they would not let me leave. She needed open heart surgery.

She needed to have the surgery soon. But despite all the help I received, it was not enough for this kind of surgery. This one requires the patient to have assisted breathing while her body remains almost frozen while the doctors repair the heart. The hourly rent for these machines is practically unaffordable.

And then, the second miracle happened. A day before I was to make the payment for the first week of hospitalization, an angel appeared in the form of a social worker. She suggested I should apply for Popular Insurance, an insurance granted by the Mexican government at that time, free of charge, to those unprotected people. And curiously, as of 2009, it also covered major surgeries.

Lucía was able to undergo surgery. The dreaded day came, and she was in the operating room for six hours. It was hard to breathe during this time that seemed to last for months. And when it was finally over, we were informed that it had been a success and that our daughter would be coming home with us.

I share all of it at this level of detail because, it happened with each of these steps at my daughter's side, I was able to realize how brave I was. I faced all my terrors, stomach, and chest tight, but head on.

In the initial chapters I shared with you how the stomach and heart are lined with layers of different metals. During these years I got the thickest layers. I became resistant to bad news and uncertainty. I faced death head on and was forced to let go, to flow, to trust, I learned to have faith.

I learned faith is opening your eyes and see what has always been there and let yourself reach out and take it. Trusting everything you need is given to you if you are able to believe what you need is given to you if you are able to believe it.

What you perceive to be true will be done.

Sometime later, I began to research the meaning of the name Lucia. Its Latin origin means LIGHT. Lucia is known as the saint of the blind and of light. There is a legend, that her name comes from the time of Emperor Galerius Maximianus, who managed to regain his sight despite having his eyes gouged out.

This little girl has undoubtedly been a source of light ever since she appeared on the map. Her presence and all the hardships we went through with her at first, restored our sight to what really matters. She took away the blindness with which we had decided to live justified in pain. And for me, she gave me the gift of living with purpose again.

With her help, I managed to get out of the hole I was living in, and she gave me back the will to fight and to move forward, for her, for me, for my two beautiful older daughters. She gave me back hope and gave me a reason to be a better human being, a better mother, the best possible version of myself.

This state of mind and the radical change in my attitude gave me all the courage I needed to restore meaning to my life. To make the decisions I had postponed for so many years, prey to fear. It gave me the clarity on the "why".

Why did I have to go through all these experiences? I understood this a little later, when I looked around me and saw so many women immersed in tremendously difficult life situations. I saw how they, as I once did, felt alone against the world and without the possibility of getting through the day.

All these women became my purpose. I understood very clearly that my work would be to accompany those who, like me, live through adverse moments. None of them should feel alone or helpless. I would be there to share with them tools and tricks to overcome adversity.

Each life is unique, with its own experiences. The questions I ask you today are:

Do you know what your purpose in life is?
What drives you?
What excites you?

I want to invite you to do an exercise of silence and internalization. Close your eyes and take a slow deep breath. Ask yourself:

What do I want?
What is it that sets my heart on fire?
What is my role on this planet?

And listen. Listen to your heartbeat. Be attentive to what it tells you. Find out what your calling is. If you don't figure it out the first time, don't worry. Do this practice regularly. It will become easier and easier for you to be still, quiet your head and listen to your Self speak to you.

Chapter 7 | Serving

Of the books I have read over the years, without a doubt, the first one that had a great impact and radical change on me was Joe Dispenza's "Stop Being You".

The first thing I learned is that where you put your attention you put your energy and that your attention relies on what you think. Therefore, if your thoughts are focused on the negative, all your energy is lost and wasted feeding the thousand-headed monster.

You will realize over time, you can produce a great deal of energy and when you use it to fuel the negative, it can grow and grow beyond measure.

In the same way, if your thoughts and your attention and therefore your energy is focused on the positive, it too can grow and grow beyond measure. The choice is yours.

The beginning of change is when you think and act beyond your present circumstances, beyond your environment.
If you remain the same as always, you cannot expect to get new results. To change your life is to change your energy to make a basic change in your mind and emotions.

Joe Dispenza says that if you want to get a new result you must suppress the habit of being the same old you and reinvent yourself. And if your mind is a product of your consciousness, then the only way to change your mind and what comes out of it is to raise your level of consciousness.

These concepts I have just shared with you seem simple, but it took me several years to understand them and, above all, to put them into practice. And of course, this was a process. I understood them little by little, one by one.

In the previous chapter I talked about how I was able to connect with my purpose and commit myself to helping all the women that life put in front of me.

But how do I begin to transform the lives of these women? By telling them about my discoveries. By sharing with them all that I have learned and that brought me out of the mire I was in.

This, my dear friends, also implies developing a genuine and selfless attitude of service. To be willing to start talking, even if at first no one listens to you. To trust in yourself again, to believe you have something to contribute. Spend many hours putting ideas in order, developing materials. Find the most appropriate means of communication to reach those to whom you want to deliver your message.

In his book, Joe Dispenza says that greatness consists of holding on to a dream, regardless of the environment where you live, of the reality in which you must live.

Since then and until today, I have created countless

writings, videos, audios in which with order and logic I have professionalized my message to reach in a clear and precise way all those women I believe I can serve.

Today I know that, as another phrase I heard attributed to Mother Teresa of Calcutta says: **He who does not live to serve, does not serve to live.**

One of the gifts that comes with connecting with your purpose, the genuine one, the one that comes from the deepest part of your being, is the imperative need to serve. To offer your time, your skills, your gifts, and your abilities in the service of others.

When this is genuine, it does not weigh you down, you do it lovingly and never get tired, because you are in connection with the endless loving energy of the universe. The more you work at it, the more energy, satisfaction, and joy you have. And the greatest gift of all and what we are sometimes not aware of is, EVERYTHING YOU GIVE, YOU GET. Life keeps nothing. Everything you give in love; you receive in abundance.

Now do you understand how important it is that your thoughts, your words, your energy, and your whole being are focused on the positive? When you can see all that there is, your life overflows with abundance and gratitude. This creates a virtuous circle that becomes expansive and contagious all around you.

Have you ever thought about what you would be willing to do, even if you didn't receive a penny in return? That activity in which you can lose yourself for hours without noticing time passing by. That thing that makes you sigh and increases your heartbeat. That thing you feel is called passion and when you connect with your passion, it brings you light and energy, because you relate to your being.

Let's do another exercise:

I invite you to pause your reading and together, again, let us together, again, let's do a practice.

Sit in a quiet place, close your eyes, take 3 slow deep breaths.

Recall moments in your life where you have felt passionate, energized, inspired. I am sure that as you remember, a smile comes to your face, a smile that is born in your heart. Feel again the harmony to which that memory takes you, feel the congruence.

It is a place where everything is well.

Just as you may have felt doing this exercise, that is how I feel in every cell of my body when I think of any activity that has to do with serving women. I visualize their smiles and their serene gaze. I imagine them full of peace and empowered. That is my driving force today. I envision my three daughters growing up, full of joy and sharing it with everyone around them. I visualize them as a light in the midst of dark environments. This is how I visualize you, who are reading these letters. As I write it, I get goosebumps and my heart is beating fast.

I want to talk to you about an important idea. Knowledge and evolution bring with them responsibility. Because once you saw the light, once you got out of the cage and spread your wings, you need to share the good news and infect your environment.

Remember we already talked about taking 100% responsibility for ourselves? Raising your consciousness involves constant self-observation. No more complaining. No more criticism. No more victimization. You commit that everything that comes out of you will be positive and constructive. No more blaming anyone for anything that happens to us. We are only responsible for our reactions to what happens and understand that we have no control over life's circumstances. We live here and now, living each moment to the fullest.

Can you imagine feeling like that? Looking like that? Interacting with the world from there? Can you imagine seeing life full of colors? Can you imagine feeling so inspired that you can inspire others?

Well, that's what personal growth work is all about, slowly but surely reaching that state of fulfillment and joy.

Today I could name countless women who live and work from that ideal state. There are famous and renowned ones and there are also those in your close circles if you know how to choose them.

Do you think these women have it all figured out? Of course not! Their lives are as full of challenges as yours and mine,

the difference is that they have already learned to live life from the center of their Being. Things keep happening, they face challenges and moments of adversity and sadness, but they live them from empathy and resilience.

And I remind you of the meaning of resilience: it is the ineffable capacity that certain people develop and that allows them to overcome the different adversities they face in their daily lives. They develop positive behaviors in face of stress, threats, or conflict. Resilient people always find a way to *rise from the ashes*.

I want to share with you three stories of women who have been a great inspiration to me. Women who, like me, have risen from the ashes.

ashes. Each one from her historical and geographical context has risen from complex and challenging lives to become a powerful example for many other women around the world.

Like them, there are many more who, through their example of courage and reconfiguration of their reality, have put their lives and experiences at the service of others.

Malala Yousafzai[2]

Malala is an activist for civil rights, especially those of women in the Swat River Valley in Pakistan, where the Taliban regime prohibits girls from attending school.

Her ideals led her to be shot in the head as she was returning by bus from school to her home in the town of Mingora. Far from backing down, the young woman took her struggle to a global level. Her work led to her being awarded the Nobel Peace Prize in 2014. At only seventeen years of age, she became the youngest person to receive this award.

Maya Angelou[3]

Writer, singer, actress, poet, screenwriter, dancer, director, prostitute, cook and civil rights activist are some of the things Maya Angelou became. Her life story is one replete with hard work, but most of all courage, perseverance, and the ability to respond in the face of great adversity.

She was known as "Dr. Maya Angelou" even though she never earned a college degree. Since the first publication of one of her seven autobiographies, she never ceased to amaze the world and her legacy has served as an inspiration to all types of communities, mainly African Americans.

---

2   United Nations (2017). Peace Messengers. United Nations. https://www.un.org
3   Russo, Fabiana (2020). The inspiring life of sublime Maya Angelou. Tentulogo. https://tentulogo.com

Oprah Winfrey [4]

Oprah Winfrey is both a woman and a black woman, yet she has been recognised as the most influential woman of her generation.

She grew up amidst the rural poverty of Mississippi and Milwaukee with her maternal grandmother, Hattie Mae Lee. Lee. She was so poor that she wore dresses made of potato sacks, which provoke mocking from other children. She was the victim of sexual abuse and a rape at age 14 from which she became pregnant. Her son was born prematurely and died shortly after birth.

She is an American journalist, television host, producer, actress, entrepreneur, philanthropist, and book reviewer. Every human being can be an instrument of service wherever he or she is. Service is an attitude, and it comes from the depths of your heart when you are connected to your purpose.

---

4   Tentulogo (2020). Oprah Winfrey, the most powerful woman of her generation. Tentulogo. https://tentulogo.com

Chapter 8 | Balance

Balance in the different spheres of our life is part of the great work we need to do to live in fullness. This task may seem simple but within the diversity of human characters, social and economic realities, personalities and tastes, this balance can be affected in many ways.

When I got married, I was fortunate to be able to dedicate a few years to home life and to planning and preparing for our family life. Since I married very young, I decided that the issue of children should wait and so we did. I lived a full and fun married life for eight years.

So, when the time came to start this family, we had already taken the time to bond as a couple and we were ready.
But as I have been telling you, things were not so simple. After many unsuccessful attempts to get pregnant, I underwent several treatments to achieve it. We spent many months in this carnival of doctors, tests, monitoring, etc.
After several previous losses, I finally got pregnant with that beautiful baby that I had the privilege of carrying for eight months and that, as I told you in another chapter, decided not to be born.

Every event we live through affects our balance in some way and it is hard work to return to it.

Mainly because when our emotions are involved this task becomes more complex.

A year after that loss I became pregnant again with my eldest daughter. I lived the months of greatest happiness, longing and fulfillment I had ever experienced. I dedicated myself to taking care of myself and making sure that this time things would go well. And it did. We had a beautiful daughter. With huge blue eyes and a beautiful smile. Her arrival healed all the sadness in our hearts, and we began a new life as a family.

Eight months after her birth, boom! I became pregnant again with my second daughter. That great project that had bankrupted us was just beginning and, sooner rather than later, we found ourselves in the middle of the hurricane that blew everything away.

Among many difficulties but very grateful, we received this beautiful daughter who came to complete the family we had dreamed of. That showed in advertising perfect pictures.

We already had our family, but the situation of bankruptcy led us to a more than complex economic situation and since then we started this race for survival.

Let me fast forward a few years later, to the year of the Apocalypse that I told you about in the first chapter. Being alone and 100% responsible for my three daughters, I needed to make big decisions and provide myself with a more stable economic life.

So, my dearest best friend offered me a job in her company, earning a salary that undoubtedly took me out of the state of emergency in which I had remained for the previous six years.

This step was extremely complicated and very painful because I had to give up my life as a present mom to become an executive. I organised my daughters' lives so that they would spend as much time as possible at school in activities and someone would take them home, where I would reunite with them late at night.

The little girl, daughter with special needs, was left in the care of the woman who for years had worked with me in cleaning and supported me taking care of my daughters. She had lived through the whole debacle with me and knew how important she was to me, my little girl. So she offered to take care of her while I worked.

Once my new reality was organized and with a hole in my heart, I began my office life. I had a hard time getting back into the ring. I became familiar with what was going on in the outside world: clients, negotiations, work meetings, new colleagues, finances and accounting. In short, a whole world I had been far from.

The first few weeks I thought my head was going to explode. I had such a hard time understanding processes and terminology. There were days when I literally felt like my eyelashes were on fire. I couldn't process one more piece of information.

I would return home to meet my daughters and attend to all their needs, mainly emotional. How difficult it was not to be able to be with them!

And in this tornado I lived the next six years. Years full of experiences and professional growth. I learned so many things and became very good at what I did. Once I got the hang of it, I really liked the executive life. I started dressing sophisticated, taking care of my image and looking very professional.

After a few years, it didn't hurt so much not to be with my daughters, I could even say that I liked the fact that I didn't have so many responsibilities at home. I did not go back to cooking, washing a single dish, or any other housekeeping activity. I only paid the bills and the salary of the person who filled that vacancy.

I must confess, and today I can't believe that, at some point I felt that way. At times I thought that my life would be much more comfortable and simpler this way, alone, working in the executive world.

And I left aside my affections, my greatest loves, which are my three daughters. Now that I can see it in the light of experience, I understand that I was extremely tired from all the years I lived wrapped up in adversity, madness, and illness. I certainly needed a break. A pause. A time for me.

During those years I went to all kinds of psychological and spiritual therapies, family constellations, consciousness development groups, self-care, spas, massages, and anything that would help me remember who I was.

I resumed the habit of reading and little by little I was forcing my brain to activate, to process all kinds of information and I became a human again and not just pieces.

And my daughters, you may ask. They dedicated themselves to school and to learning to be alone. To take care of all their things, their schoolwork, and their affective needs. To some extent they learned to live without me, but they were incomplete. They had already been left without their father, who during all those years experienced several relapses of his illness that led him to be hospitalized. The recoveries were long and tedious, and it affected my daughters very much to know that their father was living that reality.

It happened that one day when I was coming back from a weekend work trip, I had the opportunity to stay at home on a Monday. That day I sat down at the table to share a meal with my daughters when they came home from school.

My oldest daughter said to me: Mommy, it's been so many years since we sat down together for a meal on a Monday, how nice it feels! (First heartache). I didn't know what to say, I was silent and could only hug her.

After a while she told me: "They sent you a message in Lucia's notebook, they ask that you please don't miss it.
I took the notebook and it said:
Ma'am, I know you are the busiest woman in this world, but it would be very worthwhile for you to take a moment to sit down with Lucia and see what she can do.

Surprised, but not giving it much importance, I sat down at the table with her and asked her: What is it that you know how to do my girl, tell me! She opened her notebook and wrote her name, in clear, legible handwriting. She turned back a few pages and read me what it said.

My daughter with Down's Syndrome could read and write! Did you know it? ME NEITHER!

I felt as if a bucket of cold water had fallen on my head. My chest heaved and the tears started to flow. I hugged her very tightly and told her how proud I was of her.

My world turned upside down in a second. I began to question everything. What had I been doing? How was it possible that I was oblivious to all this wonder? This daughter of mine to whom I had dedicated so many years, so many sleepless nights, for whom I had asked so much of heaven to let me keep her and take care of her. I had her in complete oblivion.

If she alone, with very little vigilance and support, had accomplished this feat, what could she not accomplish with my help? My whole life flashed before my eyes that night. I could not fall asleep and I cried and cried. I felt like the worst human being on the face of the earth.

The next morning, I got up early and went to work. Midmorning, I stood up, walked into the office of the company director, and handed in my resignation.

Everyone around me was stunned by my decision. It was like taking a leap into the void. How was I going to support my family without that job? It seemed like an act of irresponsibility by all accounts.
I didn't care what other people thought. My family and their well-being were the most important thing.

That afternoon I sat down with my older daughters and told them what was going on. I told them how much I longed to be their mom again. To know them up close. To share their joys and fears. To prepare food for them. To be able to be with them during the vacations and do activities together. To be a family again.

They were delighted with my decision and told me: Even if we eat lentils for six months and we have a hard time, but we will be together.

My soul returned to my body and this time I lived my life at home from another place. Standing on my feet again. Recovered physically, emotionally, and spiritually. So began a new and wonderful stage in my life.

I have told you about the two great extremes I experienced in my adult life. The first was to dedicate myself 100% to giving everything I had to my family and to completely forget about myself. To stop taking care of myself as a woman, to stop growing and learning. To have as my only objective to give and take care of others. The second, to leave my home life after having separated from my husband, after 17 years of marriage and a few more before getting married.

I threw myself back into the working life and put aside my daughters and my life as a housewife, with all that it entailed.

It is only now, in recent years that I was able to find the balance. Once I experienced the consequences of tipping the scales only to one side and then only to the other, I became aware that a full and complete life must necessarily be balanced.

It is vitally important that in your day-to-day life you try to consider the following areas:

Family and friends
Love and partner
Growth and learning
Spirituality and peace
Money and finances
Career and work
Community living
Leisure and fun
Health and physical activity
Environment and ecological awareness

Throughout the pages of this book, we have been reviewing step by step the elements that are part of a process of awakening consciousness and the necessary evolution and changes that this brings to your life.
I have combined each of them in a series of areas that make up the 8 steps of the Valkyrie Code.

You will understand better them in the following chapters in which I talk about them in detail.

At the end of these pages, I share with you the meaning of each of the symbols that you will find in different parts of this book and mainly in each step of this method. Most of them have their origin in the times of the Vikings and the Celtic culture.

The Vikings have their origin in the Germanic peoples that inhabited Scandinavia in the Medieval Era. Specifically, they were peoples who lived in this region of Scandinavia between the years 750 and 1100 approximately.

The symbols of the Valkyrie Code are runes, which formed the writing system of the Vikings and various Nordic peoples. They are symbols and signs with alphabetic but also religious function. They were used to convey messages and leave records and as part of worship of the gods[5]. (At the end of the book you will find the precise meaning of each of them).

---

5   Fretes, Federico. (2018) Viking Civilization. Historiando. https://www.historiando.org

1. Self-knowledge (Perth)
2. Responsibility (Dagaz)
3. Habits (Uruz)
4. Balance (Sowulo)
5. Perseverance (Turisaz)
6. Purpose (Mannoz)
7. Service (Raidha)
8. Personal Growth (Berkana)

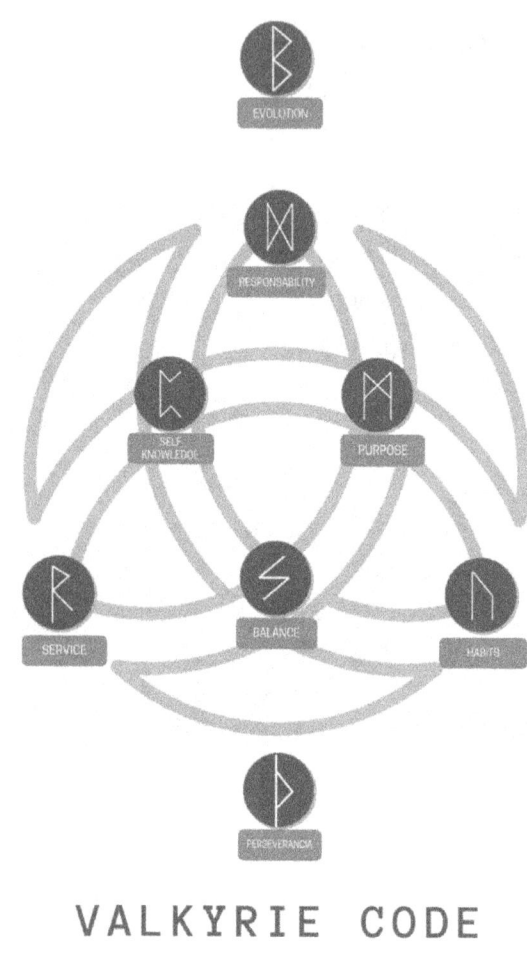

Figure 1: Valkirye Code

Chapter 9 | Decision

Every day you see people for whom everything seems to be going well, as if nothing is wrong. Life flows without any obstacle or opposition. You see them happy and enjoying the joys of their success.

At some point in my life I used to compare myself with these people and of course, from my position as a victim, I would think: Everything has gone wrong for me. If only luck would smile on me a little, I could take advantage of it and improve my situation.

Today I know none of this is real. There are no such things as 100% happy people. Nor are successful people just there, smiling and enjoying their abundance. Nor is anyone's life miserable because of bad fortune.

Today I know that success is the result of many failures from which you get up again, each time with a little more experience. The important thing is
that when you fall, you fall forward.

Almost all worthwhile things in life involve effort, determination and overcoming your fears. The point is that there is no specific class where they can teach you how to overcome fears. There are many techniques to identify them, to locate in which moment of your life each one of them settled in your mind. But overcoming them is your task alone.

In my walk I have realized that the people who manifest more fears are those who as children felt unprotected, alone in adverse situations, without support or support and those who felt humiliated for various reasons. These people, in adulthood, relive that primary fear they felt in childhood when they are faced with an adverse situation in the present.

It is not that today you do not have the possibility to face the challenges or that you do not have the capacity to solve them. Fears, from the subconscious, simply paralyze us and prevent us from moving forward.

The news is that every single human being on the face of this earth has fears of various kinds. Fear is part of our nature. That is why it is very important to work on yourself, to know yourself, to search inside yourself to discover which are the ones that hinder you in life. **What is not seen is not identified and therefore cannot be overcome.**

In my experience, the antidote to fear is decision accompanied by action. Taking action causes us to break the paralysis caused by our fears.

Do it, and if it scares you, do it with fear. The best things in life are on the other side of fear.

If I think back, it seems to me that there hasn't been a situation in my life where I haven't felt fear. On many occasions I have made decisions and done things with tears in my eyes, my stomach in knots and my legs shaking. Sometimes I've had to close my eyes when I did it and felt like I was throwing myself into the void, but the reasons for doing it have been greater than my fears.

When you have children, you become much more fearful. You see them, so fragile and dependent on you that it is overwhelming. Their life depends entirely on your care, guidance, nurturing and you must save them a thousand and one times from imminent danger.

But children also strengthen your will and drive you to action, because the great love you have for them makes you become a wonder woman full of superpowers when necessary. The heroine in you comes out from the depths and you resolve automatically. As if all the ancestral maternal energy suddenly possesses you and gives you the answers you need to get ahead.

When my youngest daughter was a baby and we had already managed to get through the heart surgery and the long recovery, it seemed that everything was finally all right. One afternoon, when I was working in my dining room while she was taking a nap with her daddy, I began to hear her coughing.

- What's wrong," I shouted. There was no answer. I got up from my chair in a hurry and went into the room to find my baby with a panicked look on her face and unable to breathe. She was choking.

I picked her up. Her little face was full of little purple dots caused by suffocation.

-What's happening," I shouted louder. Her dad just watched me, not knowing what to do.

I had never taken first aid courses, but at that moment, for some reason I remembered every TV show I had ever seen, magazine articles, videos. Everything I had ever seen regarding first aid for a choking condition.

I tapped her on the back, nothing. Tapping on the chest, nothing. I applied the technique of squeezing the pit of her stomach with my fist, nothing. I turned her upside down and hit her back again, nothing.

I remembered the procedure for a tracheotomy, which is an opening in the front of the neck that is done during an emergency procedure. I grabbed a pen and was determined to open a hole on her throat so she could breathe.

And then I played my last card. With her on her head, I stuck my finger down her throat and managed to touch what was obstructing the air path, it was hard and rough. I decided to hit the object and then... it came out. He had swallowed a 50-cent coin and it was just enough to clog the duct.

She took a huge gasp of air and began to cry at the top of her lungs and I with her. We hugged and cried for almost an hour until we regained our composure.

I couldn't stop thinking: so many tests, so much effort, therapies and surgeries for her to end up dying for a coin? There was no chance. And I could only be grateful. Thankful for this new opportunity.

This experience showed me that when you are a decided person and it is a life or death situation, your whole system plays in your favor. You produce adrenaline, your brain is activated at a much higher percentage than it normally does and I am sure that also all your ancestors in heaven come to assist you to overcome that moment of emergency. At least that's how I felt that day.

Many times in your life, your destiny will depend on the decisions you make, the small ones and the big ones. As we have already discussed in previous chapters, when you become 100% responsible for you, you realize it is you, in your free will, who has the reins of your life and therefore only you can modify everything that you do not like, that does not make you happy, that does not fulfill you.

I have had to make big decisions in my life: what career to study, to get married or not, when to have children, to move to another city, to open a business and invest all my patrimony, to take my husband to a psychiatrist, to put him in a Mental Health Institute, to save the lives of my three daughters at different times, to separate and put an end to my marriage, to leave my young daughters to start a new life, to start a new business and to invest all my patrimony. I left my job to return to my daughters' side, started a business, bet on my dreams, started my podcast Mujer a

Prueba de Balas (Bulletproof Woman), wrote this book you have in your hands.

Your life is and will be full of decisions to make. That is why it is so important that you raise your level of consciousness, that you know yourself, that you learn to live here and now, and that you are present in your life every minute, that you do not miss it by living regretting the past or anxious about the future.

Life is happening here, today, now, in this very moment. The higher the level of awareness, the better the decision making.

If you want your life to flow, to be able to live in fullness, joy and peace, live each moment as if it were the first, as if it were the last, as if it were the only one.

Don't wait for a fateful diagnosis or a tragedy or loss to happen. tragedy or loss that will make you really appreciate what you do have, what you are, and then you will be able to see that you are then you will be able to see that you are full of blessings and gifts. blessings and gifts.

You can live this reality of fullness right now. this moment.

IT IS YOUR DECISION.

I want to give you a gift that was once given to me. I am going to give you a set of affirmations so that you can repeat them every morning.

You can copy them and paste them on your bathroom mirror so you can read and remember them every day. Or you can take one with you and repeat it throughout the day and the next day another one and so on.

Focusing your attention, thoughts, and energy on them can make a big difference in your perception and it all has to do with bless. The word bless ("bendecir" in Spanish) comes from two Latin roots: bene, which means good or good and dicere, which means to say or mention. So, it is speaking to wish good to people, things, or events. Dedicate yourself to spreading the good word.

AFFIRMATIONS

I see the good around me.
I am willing to see the good in every experience.
I am surrounded by blessings, and I am determined to see them.
My whole Being vibrates with love, joy and peace.
It is my right and my responsibility to be a blessing to my world.
My smile is a blessing.
There can be so much love in me that I can heal the world.
I put my heart and mind in the present to bless it.
When I bless my world, I receive blessings back.
I bless the one who caused me pain and let healing in.

As I bless, I become aware of my role in my personal transformation.
I bless the process of entering myself and knowing myself.
Blessing takes me from the mundane to the sacred.
I bless my present moment and I am here and now.
No one is exempt from receiving a blessing
Something happens to my fear when I bless.
By blessing, I create and co-create the world around me.
To bless I must first overcome my resistances.
My blessings are treasures that I can place well.
I am just a conduit of blessing.

Work every day on being a determined person. Willpower is the unwavering determination to carry a task, which you yourself have decided and set for yourself, through to completion.

Persistence and perseverance are the secret to make your dreams and desires come true.

It takes guts to reach the Glory. Blessing and gratitude are your greatest tools.

You will be amazed at how quickly the Universe will respond once you have made up your mind.

Be a determined person!

Chapter 10 | Perseverance

The day I began to walk alone, as a grown woman, a mother of three and leaving a lifetime behind, when my destiny and that of my daughters truly depended only on me, that day I began to see the profound value and importance of perseverance.

I realized how many years I had lived in austerity and survival only. With no greater aspirations than to get to the end of the day without stumbling or without something to regret.

The first step I took was to start reading. I had given up the habit I had been so passionate about for many years, too many. My brain was all out of shape. I had a hard time retaining data, information, remembering what I had read. Most of the time when I read, I would fall asleep without getting past three pages.

Any substantial change in our lives takes time, modifying our habits into those that are good for us, first requires us to be aware of everything we do every day that does not add up or help us.

Eating habits, physical habits, emotional habits, we are full of habits, good and bad. Small decisions we make at every moment. These habits can lead us to a functional, healthy, and productive life or to a destructive, tired and detrimental to the evolution of our Being.

In my experience, the path to improvement begins by accepting that we are bad in some, several, or all areas. Accepting it and recognizing that we need to do something about it is the first step.

Looking for literature, videos, audio books, movies or any source that can inspire us is the next step. Look for life stories that inspire and show us that anything is possible.

Another of the first books that fell into my hands and changed my vision completely was The Compound Effect, by author Darren Hardy. In it, he describes and demonstrates how small changes in our habits have an important and far-reaching effect in the long run.

Over the past eight years I have experienced a series of ups and downs. For a while I achieved some economic stability after so many years of anguish, lack and tastelessness. My office job gave me that stability, at least for a while, the one I needed to put my soul and mind back in order and become a *normal* person again.

The point here, and if you remember what I have told you so far, was that after my painful awakening I had found my voice again: my purpose, my vocation. That inner fire that had remained extinguished for so many years and that, being lit again, would not leave me in peace. It would not allow me to follow a path that would not lead me to my personal fulfillment. And the office life, no matter how much stability it gave me, was not my path, nor did it lead me to my fulfillment and the fulfillment of my dreams.

At first with fear and uncertainty but determined that my life was about more than just getting to the end of the day. I began to grow. To take all the courses, workshops, therapies, webinars, or study groups that were available on the internet.

Working on your personal growth opens your eyes to things you have forgotten along the way. It helps you to re-evaluate yourself and to realize how, when you are not aware of who you are, many of the actions you take daily are done from the automatic, without really reflecting on them.

Becoming aware of the things that were really important to me brought with it the responsibility to move in that direction.

Of all the things I may have longed for over the previous fifteen years, I realized that my greatest longing was for peace. It became the end to seek and work toward.

For me, working on finding my peace became my priority and my new mission. Modifying and adapting the life you lead from unconsciousness to one that does not depend on anyone else to be full and complete is a task that must be done every day.

The definition of persevering says that it is to remain firm and constant in a way of being or acting. To stay on the path, you have decided to take, even when obstacles and trials arise. When it comes to becoming a better version of yourself, it is first necessary to become aware of all the bad habits you have accumulated and change them little by little for better ones.

What has been the hardest thing for me is to persevere, to finish the things I start. I was so used to letting my emotions rule me, that if something did not turn out the way I liked or according to my expectations, I always use to give up what I had started.

I told you about the day I made the decision to leave my office life to go back home to my daughters. Without a doubt, it was the best decision I ever made.

By the time that day came, I was a little over a year into a direct sales company. Everything there was new to me, the way I worked, the way I set goals that depended 100% on my performance and my perseverance.

I worked this venture in parallel to my office life and when I decided to leave that job, it became my only source of income. Then I experienced the consequences of making a hasty decision. But even today, I do not regret having done it because it taught me to work by objectives and to keep myself in a state of constant learning.

During the last few years, I have lived through stages of stability and abundance and many of challenges and austerity. I have learned that the road to success and fulfillment does not go in a straight line. It has ups, downs, and sometimes unforeseen deviations. The important thing is to move towards a goal. A goal that excites you, that sets your heart on fire, that becomes your reason to get up when for some reason you fall.

To persevere is to do things, even if sometimes you don't feel like it. Keep trying, even if you face obstacles. To fight all your inner voices that tell you that you are not going to make it, that you do not deserve it, that you are not worth it, that nobody believes in you, that they will criticize and judge you.

Persevere is to wake up every morning with a goal to achieve, whether big or small, but that brings you a little closer to fulfilling your dream. Sometimes you will take big steps and sometimes very small ones, what counts is that you do not stop moving forward.

It is worthwhile to work on adding habits that bring you physical and mental well-being, that make you feel healthy, happy, and full of energy. At first you will feel uncomfortable, because you will be moving out of your comfort zone, but I assure you that every change, big or small, is worth it.

If you have not yet become aware of your habits, I invite you to stop for a moment and analyze:

The time and the way you wake up.
What you devote your first thoughts of the day to.
How you eat and the type of food in your refrigerator and pantry.
What kind of attention you give to others?

How you spend your money.
How you organize your daily life.
With what attitude you face the different situations that the day brings.
How much time you spend studying, reading, watching TV, using devices.

Another book that transformed me in an important way was The 5am Club by Robin Sharma. In it he describes in detail why it is important to work on the physical, spiritual and self-actualization areas.

For the first time in my life, I got up very early. I went for a walk first and eventually started running. In my case, not for competitive purposes but to feel energized, active, with a clear mind and a better attitude. Then I meditated or prayed, and in the third instance, I worked on the project that would be my legacy, my motive, my purpose.

My life changed 180 degrees by doing these three things every morning. I stopped having headaches (I used to get them very often), I felt invigorated and happy, but above all very satisfied of doing something for me and for me. That morning hour was my gift, the time to be with me, to reflect and plan.

Today, with my head held high, I can make a long list of all the small and big things I have achieved. There have been many and today I am not even a shadow of what I was in those years of difficulty, sadness, and complaint. I have learned to be my biggest fan and cheerleader. I have learned that the most recognition I need comes from myself and that helps me to handle myself much better with others, because what I do, I don't do for anyone else, I do it for me.

Every day of your life is full of small achievements and successes. Some of them pass you by overnight. It is important to become aware of all that you DO, what you DO achieve, the love you DO give and receive. A successful life is made up of many small successes.

Stop for a moment and observe, remember, reflect on your accomplishments and successes. Start with the little ones.

Success is discovering that what you have always wanted is within you, therefore, you can set your mind to something and achieve it. This leads to a life of power, freedom, and fulfillment.

Another valuable exercise or practice you can do is to keep a journal in which you record every good thing that happens to you and that you achieve. A journal of blessings, achievements, and progress. It leads you to realize how many events you experience daily that you pass over and do not appreciate, do not value and are not grateful for.

It can be a notebook designed just for this purpose or you can keep track of it in your diary. For me it works very well to write down everything I did accomplish that day and put a check mark on it. I write down all my accomplishments and small successes even if they seem unimportant or inconsequential.

Remember what we define as success? Setting your mind to something and doing it. The sum of small daily successes can bring you to an important state of satisfaction and joy and impel you to continue along that line.

Beginning to change your mindset and attitude to one of HOW CAN IT BE POSSIBLE and SEEING WHAT YOU DO HAVE, is the most important step to begin living a fulfilling and purposeful life.

Chapter 11 | Engagement

I vividly remember all those mornings when, upon opening my eyes and after my ceremony of turning my stomach from the bile accumulated during the night, I would lie in bed staring at the ceiling, my eyes fixed on a point that told me nothing. Many times, I didn't even think, I just lived in a state of lethargy and inactivity caused by mental, physical, and soul exhaustion.

Today I understand that, basically, I felt disheartened. When the heart is sad and defeated, it is hard to get going.

In a moment of light and understanding, I saw the faces of my three daughters in front of me. Potential extraordinary human beings. I understood that no matter how I felt, they needed their mother to care for them and guide them in the years to come.

One of those mornings, I committed from the deepest part of my being to take the ship to a safe harbor, the ship of which I was now captain. I committed myself to work every day, for the rest of my life, to make this a better world for my daughters and my daughters' children.

I made a commitment to myself to work with all my might to become the best version of myself that I could be, no matter how long it took.

Some years later I realized that this commitment was not only with my daughters and myself but with every woman, who for some reason was living a situation like so many that I lived. A deep love for my gender was born in me. An immense need to see every woman full and happy, free of fear and self-confident.

I was able to see that, in this life, what makes you great is knowing you are great, valuing yourself, recognizing yourself, loving yourself and going after what you want and what you believe in.

This led me to get in touch with this purpose of finding my own voice. To believe with all my heart that, no matter what others think, I need to speak MY TRUTH.

And like those coincidences that suddenly happen when you connect with your being, I got my hands on a writing by Audre Lorde that read:

Talking will become easier and easier. And you will discover that you have fallen in love with your own vision, which you may not have known you had. And you will lose some friends and lovers and realize you don't miss them.
And new ones will find and appreciate you.... And you will finally know with a beautiful certainty there is only one thing that is more terrifying than expressing your truth. And that is, not to express it.

Little by little I regained my self-confidence. I worked on modifying my habits, one by one, especially those that obviously did not bring me well-being.

I would love to tell you that it was easy and fast, but it was not like that. It was a gradual change, and it took time, but each modification in consciousness brought a good result.

I want to share with you some of the main points on which I worked and that after the years I baptized as:

EIGHT SUPERPOWERS OF A WOMAN

1. SELF AWARENESS
Of what you are, what you have achieved and what you can achieve.
Awaken to the realization that you don't need anything outside, everything already is, has been given to you. That you just must begin to see it.

2. GRATITUDE
It is the secret weapon to change your reality into one full of abundance. It allows you to see what is there, what you do have and value it. Being grateful is the most important attitude change. It makes you aware that if you change yourself, the world changes.

3. ACCEPTANCE
Learn to flow with what is presented and be aware that the only constant is change. Whatever may happen to you is so, it is a moment, a reality that brings with it new challenges. When you manage to see problems as facts, trying not to involve emotions, you understand that the only thing you can control is your reaction to the circumstances. You have control over almost nothing.

4. RESILIENCE

It is the forced growth you get after suffering a trauma, a loss, or a shock. The ability we develop to overcome an adverse situation more quickly and easily.

The emotional strength that we develop, the attitude that derives from the survival instinct. The result of Nietzsche's well-known phrase: what does not kill you makes you stronger.

5. BELIEVE IN YOURSELF AND RESPECT YOURSELF

Work on your self-esteem. Modify the way you see yourself. Become aware of how you talk to yourself, what is your internal conversation from the moment you open your eyes until you close them. Learn to value yourself and to be your best friend and your biggest fan. If you respect yourself, others respect you.

6. BE RESOURCEFUL

Develop the ability to observe, evaluate and make use of the resources or possibilities you do have to solve any problem. To be resourceful in the best way and get out of a difficult moment and, why not, surpassing any expectation, mainly your own.

7. COOPERATE

Develop the ability to see in people their abilities and strengths, all the good that each person has from their unique being. Apply your skills for the welfare of all who may be involved.

8. SORORITY

Sorority proposes to be women united beyond ideologies, religions and cultures. It is a door that opens where we are all together. It is always to be a support for other women, understanding that if one woman improves, we all improve.

There is a phrase I read somewhere: If you invest in a woman, you have invested in the future of many generations.

I want to give you a recognition, because to begin with, you are a woman who has made the decision to read, to know other points of view, to know other life stories, like mine, to get inspiration and elements of improvement from them.

It is very worthwhile that, once again, you take a break to reflect on your own life and be honest to see what level of commitment you have, first, with yourself and then with all the people who are important to you.

Are you really clear about where your life is going?
Do you get up every morning with enthusiasm or with gloom?
What are the good habits you need to add to your life?
What are you going to do TODAY to change anything that doesn't look like what you really want?
What are you committed to?

I return for a moment to the theme of Sorority to tell you that, in any case, you are not alone. There are many, many, many other women in your situation, full of challenges and dreams, ready to team up with you to make this a better world and contribute to make your life a fulfilling and extraordinary life.

You just have to take the first step.

Chapter 12 | The Birth of a Valkyrie

Working on my way of contributing to empowerment, I have fallen deeply in love with women. I have come to understand the transcendent role of being a woman. I have been able to feel and connect with the energy that sustains this planet. I have identified the many attributes that a woman has just because she is a woman.

A few years ago, when I was in the process of defining my venture, my why and what for, in a dream, the figure of the Valkyrie appeared before me, that strong and seasoned warrior woman. I remembered that, as a child, I was called that, and I felt very identified with what she represents.

After understanding that there are women who must go into battle and play the roles of men and women without the option of surrendering and without being able to choose, as happened to me, I found in the Valkyries the image with which I identified completely.

In history, these Nordic (Viking) maidens were depicted as young and beautiful, with gleaming white arms and flowing golden hair.

Powerful women, brave warriors, beautiful and of great strength, charged with protecting the gods and beings of all the worlds of Scandinavian mythology, they rode through the skies of these worlds on great winged horses, dressed in shining and beautiful armor woven by the gods of Asgaard and wielding great spears and swords.

The mission of the Valkyries, apart from defending and protecting, was to go in search of the Viking warriors fallen in battle.

Another power of the Valkyries was their healing abilities, which they used to help the wounded who were not yet ready to leave the world of men.

The Valkyries acted under the orders of Freya, the goddess of love and fertility, however, they had their own queen, Brunhild, who led this army. She was the most powerful Valkyrie of them all, her strength was greater than that of 12 men combined.[6]

In a visualization exercise I did, I closed my eyes, and I saw myself as this powerful queen. I took a deep breath and launched a call, to the four cardinal points, summoning all the Valkyries of the North, South, East, and West to connect with this vision of contributing to the evolution of the female gender. To join me in this mission to rescue so many women who have gone and the ones remaining on the road, after their personal battles.

Some have been mortally wounded, others survive in the shadows. All of them deserve to see the light again. To heal and live their lives to the fullest.

---

6   Ribas, Ester (2019). Valkyries, the heroines of Norse mythology. Northmen Blog about Norse mythology, a journey through the northern countries. https://www.ester-ribas.com

We Valkyries are here for each other, to help each other, to nurture and support each other until each one of them gets back on their feet.

Today I call again for you to be part of this group of women who are and will be there for each other. To be able to see how, when you reach out and help another woman, the greatest benefit is yours.

Certainly, each of us has different gifts, abilities, and strengths. The first step is to identify yours:

What makes you unique?
What is your GIFT?
What is your passion?
What are you good at?
What sets your heart on fire?

The wonder of studying, expanding your knowledge, molding your criteria, and opening yourself to new ideas and possibilities is that in the end you realize that the greatest gain you can obtain and what we should all aspire to is to be happy.

I want to share with you six maxims that I came to and that I practice after all my stumbles, learnings, and life lessons.

The more you are who you are, the happier you will be.
The more you do in freedom what you love, the happier you will feel.
The less money you need, the happier you will feel.

The less you need from people, the happier you will feel.
The less attachment you have to things, the happier you will feel.
The more you learn to flow with what reality presents to you, the calmer you will live.

I have learned that the focus, motive, and root of everything we do in life must be based on love.

Love is neither given nor received, you are love. There comes a time when giving or receiving it has no relevance and we only live within and from it.

The great work that each one of us needs to do is to learn to love ourselves first.

Frida Kahlo, a Mexican painter said:
Fall in love with yourself, with life and then with whoever you want.

To give meaning to life we must work every day on being close to what motivates us and makes us move. When our sense of life emerges, people perceive it and recognize it. This happens when you are connected to your light.

Vocation is the point where your own voice meets the needs of the world.

The change of consciousness is a process, you gradually grow in wisdom and capabilities.

To live in faith and wisdom is to do so with eyes that allow you to see what has always been there and allow you to come closer to taking it.

You are always going to regret more what you didn't do than what you did do. There is no better day to start than **TODAY**, it is never too late. This is the first day of the rest of your life.

Every experience you have had up to yesterday is part of who you are, it has shaped you and it is what it is. You can look at it with nostalgia, regret and suffering or you can decide to transform it into a story of victory by focusing on all that it left behind and taught you.

Chapter 13 | Your Life Happens Today

This book has surely spoken to you in different ways. Perhaps you identified with a particular experience or saw yourself reflected in some of its paragraphs. Each person sees, receives, and assimilates from who he or she is. From their level of consciousness, understanding and knowledge.

I am sure that in some of its pages there may be a message that can serve as a light to illuminate a moment of difficulty that you may be experiencing.

Of all the messages that I want you to take away after reading this book, I will highlight the most important ones:

1. As long as things do not get really serious, we humans "get used to it", we live at the mercy of events.

2. Life happens here and now. If you are anywhere else, you are missing out on the privilege of actually living.

3. If you make the committed decision to grow. To be brave and open the door that opens inward. You will be able to know yourself and go, little by little, turning on the light in every dark corner that exists within you and that, until today have not allowed you to live happily and fully.

4. Don't wait for a fateful diagnosis, or for some tragedy or loss to happen that will make you really value what you do have, what you are, and then you will be able to see that you are full of blessings and gifts.

5. The change of consciousness is a process; you grow gradually in wisdom and capabilities.

6. To live in faith and wisdom is to do so with the eyes that allow you to see what has always been there and to allow you to come closer to taking it.

7. To begin to change your mindset and attitude into one of HOW TO DO IT is the most important step to begin to live a full and purposeful life.

8. You are your best investment, unless you think you are not a good investment.

9. If you are well, your environment is well.

10. When you change, the world changes.

11. Universal Law: as inside is outside and as outside is inside.

12. If you want your life to flow, to be able to live in fullness, joy and peace, live each moment as if it were the first, as if it were the last, as if it were the only one.

13. Do it, and if it scares you, do it with fear. The best things in life are on the other side of fear.

14. Success is discovering that what you have always wanted is within you, therefore, you can set your mind to something and achieve it. This leads to a life of power, freedom, and fulfillment.

15. Enjoy the journey and do not despair, the greatest learning can happen while you are going where you want to go.

16. Living without a purpose is like wanting to sail the sea without a compass, without a road map, without knowing where you are going. It is important that your life has meaning so that you are not at the mercy of circumstances, like a ship without a rudder.

17. Love is not given, it is. YOU ARE LOVE! And true love is born from an inexhaustible source, it never ends and there is enough to give and give away. That love is inside you, not outside.

18. We Valkyries are there for each other, to help each other, to nurture and support each other until each one of us gets back on our feet.

19. One of the gifts that comes with connecting with your purpose, the genuine one, the one that comes from the deepest part of your being, is the imperative need to serve.

20. Mother Teresa of Calcutta: He who does not live to serve, does not serve to live.

21. **Each person can be an instrument of service wherever he or she works. Service is an attitude and is born from the depths of the heart when you are connected to your purpose. when you are connected to your purpose.**

As I write this final chapter, we are in the last month of the year 2020, the year of the Covid 19 pandemic. Every human being on the face of this planet has had a radical change in the way they live, work, relate and above all how they view themselves.

In all sincerity I can tell you that each one of the experiences I have lived throughout my life and the renewed way I have of seeing things, of facing challenges, the resilience I have managed to develop, the knowledge I have acquired and the growth I have achieved, bore abundant fruits, especially this year.

I was able to realize that when you manage to live most of the time in peace without pretending to control anything and just flow with what appears, good and bad in absolute acceptance, not even a global pandemic can take you out of your center.

Challenges? I had plenty of them, but until today, they have been just that, challenges, and experiences to overcome and from which I continue to learn about myself and about everyone else.

Today, with a huge smile on my face, I can tell you that I do what I love to do, which is to tell my life stories from a place of victory and wisdom. I have left behind the eternal victim and my horror stories, which were mainly created and lived from my mind, in absolute unconsciousness and I live in fullness and gratitude for every day that I can continue to breathe and enjoy watching my daughters grow up.

I can also tell you that inner work and living in a state of consciousness is not so difficult. More than hard work it is a matter of decision. You decide to stop living full of fears and limiting beliefs. You decide to stop the judgment and negative internal conversations. You decide to see what is there and based on that see what you can do, without anguish or worry and just solve. YOU DECIDE TO BE HAPPY.

My day-to-day life today is full of richness. I can dedicate myself to what I like and what I am passionate about. I dedicate myself to give lectures, conferences, and workshops for women. Focused on a real empowerment from the Self. Among all of us we help each other to discover our own voice and to be able to speak our truth without fear and in complete freedom.

I dedicate much of my activity to support awareness, inclusion and appreciation of Down Syndrome and other disabling conditions, sharing the testimony of what has been my life with my daughter Lucia, who as she grows and develops has become a girl full of skills, virtues, and gifts to share with the world.

More than a year ago I started broadcasting a podcast I called Mujer a Prueba de Balas (Bulletproof Woman). In each of its episodes I have the fortune to interview and meet brave women who decide to share their life stories. Stories of different kinds and with different degrees of difficulty, but without a doubt, each one of them full of inspiration and wisdom.

Today I work doing what I love and collaborate with many other entrepreneurs who, like me, are giving shape and voice to their own dreams and with whom I have interesting points of contact.

My deep love for literature has also led me to collaborate with renowned New York Times bestselling writers, supporting them with the translation of different books from English to Spanish and vice versa. This has been an invaluable source of wealth, as I have studied their work, their proposals, and their life formulas in detail. To a great extent this has inspired me to finally decide to write this book that you have in your hands.

I am deeply grateful for so many blessings that I enjoy every day, for the abundance and prosperity that I am able to see and experience. For the opportunity to meet so many valuable people in so many countries around the world. People with whom I collaborate in various ways and who, if it were not for this pandemic I have experienced, I would not have met.

All crises are gifts wrapped in sandpaper, but gifts, nonetheless. It is up to each one of us to discover the richness they will bring to our lives.

I have another great dream. To create schools so that the more than thirteen million girls around the world who do not have the opportunity to study because of gender or social and cultural beliefs, can do so. I am certain that the change and evolution that the female gender has been crying out for several decades cannot really happen unless it comes from the grassroots. May we succeed in strengthening the spirit of so many girls who, in a few years, will be the women who will take over from us in this awareness that we are all equal, we are all valuable and we are all necessary.

Perhaps this work will take us several generations and I will not be around to see its fruits, but I have the faith and certainty that each woman is finally connecting with a light that is more powerful than any darkness:

THE LIGHT OF HER OWN BEING.

I want to thank you for the time you have dedicated to share with me and to be part of my life by reading these pages. And I also want to invite you to be part of the change of mentality and way of life that our land and our society need so much.

It starts today, it starts with you. I remind you again that the only thing you can control is what happens inside you and your reaction to what happens outside, the rest is just life.

Your life is happening right now, and you have the opportunity to enjoy each day aware that it is a gift.
When you go to bed at night, you can rest in the magic of a day well lived and be thankful for all the little miracles you witness each day.

I embrace you wherever you are and wish you a life full of awareness, richness and fullness lived from your BEING.

MAKE IT EXTRAORDINARY

Epilogue

The journey towards the reunion with my Self has been quite an adventure and along the way I have encountered elements of great significance. Symbols that have spoken to me deeply and with which I have identified myself over the years.

Each one has a reason for being and for being part of this content. They have become my banner and my reminders of all that I have managed to overcome when I suddenly lose my way again.

Celtic culture and the Vikings have been with me all my life and I find them enigmatic, exciting and at the same time familiar. I told you that since I was a child, I was called the Valkyrie. Closing my eyes and visualizing myself as one of them gives me an energy that comes from deep inside and that has no beginning or end, it just is.

This is why I want to share with you the meanings of each of the symbols I use throughout the book and in my life, because if you really identify with this journey and feel the call, you too can be part of this army of Valkyrie women, join the cause of bringing a message of strength, resilience and recovery to other women who may find themselves in an unfavorable or adverse situation.

The process of change and evolution that I have shared with you through each chapter of this book are combined in the Valkyrie Code, which consists of 8 internal processes that if you work them one by one, with patience, perseverance and dedication can help you achieve integral growth, so that you can live happy, full and fulfilled every day that you are fortunate enough to inhabit this planet.

I make a call to all the Valkyries of the four cardinal points to make a virtuous and constructive energy circle in favor of our gender and together we work to make this world a better world.

You can download each of these symbols as images on my website and have them present in your daily life, place them in the mirror where you look at yourself every morning and evoke all the strength they have. That is my gift to you in gratitude for your time and for joining this crusade.

Enter to my website:
https://paulamzaragoza.com/descargas

From my library to you

Finally, I want to give you the list of books that have given me the most. Some of them have literally changed my life. I am sure that among their pages you will find a lot of light for the road.

The wealth is within you, James Allen

The Four Agreements, Miguel Ángel Ruiz Macías

Cultivating My Inner Mentor, Valentín Méndez

Stop Being You, Joe Dispenza

Think and Grow Rich, Napoleon Hill

As a man thinks, so is his life, James Allen

The Power to Change Everything, Yehuda Berg

The 5am Club, Robin Sharma

The Compound Effect, Darren Hardy

The Power of Now, Eckhart Tolle

Synchro Destiny, Deepak Chopra

Letting Go: The Path to Liberation, David R. Hawkins

XI The Eleventh Commandment, Thou shalt not kill your dreams, Mario A Rosen

The Shack, William Paul Young

The War of Art, Stephen Pressfield

About the Author

Paula is a Journalist. Communication Intelligence Specialist. Radio broadcaster and writer.

Creator of the Podcast Mujer a Prueba de Balas (Bulletproof Woman), dedicated to the accompaniment and empowerment of women.

Single mother of 3 daughters, the youngest, a girl with Down Syndrome, which has led her to become a specialist on the subject.

Within the editorial field, dedicated to proofreading, Spanish-English-Spanish translations. Content development, copywriting and mastery of digital communication platforms.

Dedicated to giving lectures, conferences and workshops on Personal Leadership and Empowerment through consciousness and Communication Intelligence.

A woman in constant evolution, passionate about working with women and supporting them in finding their own voice and empowerment through manifesting their unique Self, their virtues and strengths.

Final Comments

My first adventure as a writer took place not long ago when I felt an inescapable call to be part of HOW TO ACTUALLY DO IT, and to contribute to the strengthening of the female gender from the elevation of their consciousness and empowerment. But what does it mean to live in consciousness?

For me, it means to stop blaming what happens outside for our bad fortune and misfortune. It means "taking the bull by the horns" and looking inward and starting to know yourself. To be much more loving to yourself. Recognizing that every step you have taken has put you where you are and that you are the only one who can get you out of it.

It means knowing that you have been the hero of your own life, knowing that you have always done the best you could with what you knew and had. It is knowing that you are a survivor of your own story, that you have always done well, and above all things, that today you can do better, from your own dreams and desires, from your power. The power of LOVE.

Paula M Zaragoza

I invite you to also take the opportunity to read my MANIFESTO ON A NEW FEMINISM: Women Empowered from the Self.

You can also find it in digital version on Amazon at the following link: https://amzn.to/3na5F5r

Additional Resources

Celtic Triquette

This symbol has been interpreted in different ways but all of them are related to the importance of the number three. Thus, it is possible to understand this symbol as a representation of the past, the present and the future.

Similarly, it could be understood as a symbol of birth, life and death; childhood, maturity and old age.

On a more spiritual plane, this symbol can represent the body, mind and spirit. Some traditions have also related it to the earth and its main elements: earth, water and air. It also had meanings such as change, harmony of the world and eternal learning. This is a Celtic lunar sign that has form.

This is a Celtic lunar sign that has the shape of a helix, and includes a ring connecting the three loops that represent the union and the cycle of life, also to eternity.

It is attributed with properties of renewal, both spiritual and physical, and important vital energy.

It is a symbol of positive light that attracts an important force of renewal and personal and spiritual evolution. It is also closely connected to the fertility of women, because the Celts attached great importance to the gift of giving life that they possess.

Dragonfly Symbolism

The dragonfly, in almost all parts of the world, symbolizes the change in perspective of self-realization, mental, emotional maturity and deep understanding of the meaning of life. Its flight across the water represents an act of going beyond what is on the surface and looking into the deeper implications and aspects of life.

The dragonfly's agile flight and ability to move in all directions exudes a sense of power and balance, something that only comes with age and maturity.

The dragonfly normally lives most of its life as a nymph, not as an adult, in which state it lives for only about two months. The adult dragonfly does everything in this short time. This lifestyle symbolizes and exemplifies the virtue of living in the moment and living life to the fullest, being aware of who you are, where you are, what you are doing, what you want.

Valkyrie Code
8 Principles to be a Bulletproof Woman

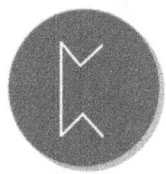

PERTH
Self-knowledge
Initiation, rebirth, powerful forces of change.

MANNAZ
Purpose
Intuition, inner light, discovery, breakthrough.

DAGAZ
Self, Manifestation of the Self, divine union, learning to relate to oneself.

URUZ
Habits
Strength, primary creative force.

SOWULO
Balance
The whole, complete, totality.

RAIDHA
Service
Path, journey, trip, solar chariot.

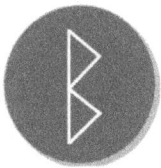

BERKANA
Evolution
Growth, fertility, birth, new life.

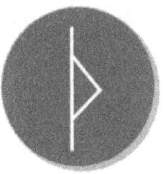

TURISAZ
Perseverance
Gateway, opening, path, regeneration.

www.ingramcontent.com/pod-product-compliance
Lightning Source LLC
Chambersburg PA
CBHW050250120526
44590CB00016B/2295